Contents

Work relief in Vermont

PICKAXE
AND
PENCIL

*References
for the
Study of the WPA*

Compiled by

MARGUERITE D. BLOXOM

*Bibliography Section
General Reading Rooms Division*

Library of Congress   Washington   1982

Library of Congress Cataloging in Publication Data

Bloxom, Marguerite D.
  Pickaxe and pencil.

  Includes index.
  Supt. of docs. no.: LC 1.2:P58
  1. United States. Works Progress Administration
—Bibliography.   2. Public service employment—
United States—Bibliography.   I. Library of Congress.
General Reading Rooms Division. Bibliography Sec-
tion.   II. Title.
Z7164.P97B58   [HD5713.6.U54]   016.3530083'4   81–607135
ISBN 0–8444–0384–9   AACR2

Photographs illustrating this publication
are from the collections of the
National Archives and Records Services,
Washington, D.C.

Preface

The WPA—originally the Works Progress Administration and later the Work Projects Administration—represented a social experiment in which money from the federal government was expended in work relief for millions of unemployed Americans in the hope of reviving a depressed economy. Definitive conclusions about its success cannot be drawn, however, as defense mobilization for World War II cured the Depression before the WPA program could be completed.

Today, nearly forty years after the termination of the program, curiosity about WPA projects, their problems and achievements, appears to be growing. This bibliography was prepared to help meet the need for information about what the WPA was, what it did, and what became of it.

References are primarily to books (including pamphlets) and to articles from scholarly journals and popular magazines. For the most part unpublished dissertations have not been included in individual sections (with the exception of the Federal Music Project where a dearth of other material made the inclusion of dissertations seem desirable) but a list of relevant dissertations appears in Appendix I. References to newspaper articles, congressional documents, manuscript collections, or unpublished sources are not included, but a few archival guides are listed. In most sections material is divided into "At the Time"—items which were published in 1943 or earlier—and "Looking Back"—entries which were published after 1943 and include recent work. It is believed that two different perspectives on the WPA are reflected by this division.

No attempt was made in this bibliography to describe the quantities of published and unpublished WPA items now housed in the Library of Congress, except in instances where such material was discussed in published accounts or listed in bibliographies. John Cole (no. 315) noted that in 1941 more than 80 Library employees were engaged in receiving and sorting boxes and crates of WPA papers forwarded from state projects and elsewhere."Hundreds of WPA publications were added to the Library's classified collections and many unfinished documents, indexes, and working materials were absorbed into specialized collections. For example, the ex-slave narratives went to the Rare Book Division; additional ex-slave documentation, along with hundreds of folklore recordings and ethnic studies to the Archive of Folk Song; an index of American composers to the Music Division; photographs and posters to the Prints and Photographs Division; and the Manuscript Division became the repository of several sets of transcripts and unpublished manuscripts." Much of this material is increasingly being made accessible for research.

The compiler wishes to extend thanks to Ruth S. Freitag and Judith P. Austin for their support, advice, and editorial assistance. The McKeldin Library at the University of Maryland, College Park, proved to be a valuable source of serials that were missing elsewhere.

Key to Symbols

DLC
Cataloging currently under way

Folk
Archive of Folk Song

GRR Bibl
General Reading Rooms Division, Bibliography Sectior

Micro
Microform Reading Room

MRR Alc
Main Reading Room Reference Collection

MRR Ref Desk
Main Reading Room Reference Alcoves

N&CPR
Newspaper and Current Periodical Room

Rare Bk Coll
Rare Book Collection

WPA workmen at Washington National Airport, 1939

I

The Depression, the New Deal, and Work Relief

Rarely does a decade seem so clearly delineated by markers of social and economic change as was the Great Depression of the thirties, for it began with the stock market panic of October 1929 and ended in December 1941 when the Japanese attack on Pearl Harbor thrust the United States into World War II. The period was one of depression, not only of the economy but of the spirit of the people, as unemployment and the resultant poverty engulfed the land.

Caroline Bird observed that "the wake of the Crash moved like a tidal wave, wrecking parts of the economy that seemed far removed from the turbulent market on Wall Street." Prices fell, factories closed, falling grain prices ruined farmers, mortgages were foreclosed. Everywhere people were hungry and homeless.

It was difficult at first to grasp the immensity of the problem. Hoover administration officials hoped the situation was a temporary one that would soon correct itself. Republicans continued to assert that any man willing and able to work could find a job if he looked; failure was the fault of the individual.

In 1932 Franklin D. Roosevelt was overwhelmingly elected President bringing with him hope, enthusiasm, and the reassurance that the country had nothing to fear "but fear itself." He promised a new deal, a policy of optimism that would send federal money and influence down new paths to experiment with new programs. The government was going to be an active participant in the revival of the economy.

From the beginning, the concept of work relief rather than direct aid (the dole) was an intrinsic part of the planning of the new administration. From the legislation of the National Industrial Recovery Act of 1933 came the Public Works Administration, headed by Harold Ickes, with a program that would put the unemployed to work on major construction projects, such as dams, highways, and public buildings. Since these projects required planning and justification, they were slow in starting, while the needs of the unemployed were pressing.

Into the gap moved the Federal Emergency Relief Administration which had been created about the same time and placed under the direction of Harry Hopkins. Its initial function was to coordinate relief efforts at the state level, but it quickly took a leadership role in designing proposals for new, sometimes temporary, work programs. For example, the Civil Works Administration was organized under FERA aegis in 1933 with the announced goal of employing four million people within thirty days and keeping them working until spring at almost any useful jobs available. FERA was also concerned with work relief programs for the "white collar" worker, and many of its pioneer efforts broke ground for later WPA arts projects.

The following references were selected to provide an introduction to the period and its beginnings of experimentation with work relief. Later sections will explore the many projects of the WPA in greater detail.

"At the time": Pre-1943 Publications

001

Abbott, Edith. "Work or maintenance": a federal program for the unemployed. Social service review, v. 15, Sept. 1941: 520-532.   HV1.S6, v. 15

Work relief must be administered by the federal government in order to avoid the confusion that might be generated by state and local management.

002

Allen, Frederick L. Since yesterday; the nineteen-thirties in America. New York, Harper, 1940. xiv, 362 p. facsims., plates, ports.   E741.A66

003

Anderson, Nels. The right to work. New York, Modern Age Books, [c1938] illus.
                               HD3885.A65
An analysis of work relief by the director of the Section on Labor Relations, Works Progress Administration.

004

Burns, Arthur E., and Edward A. Williams. Federal work, security, and relief programs. Washington, U.S. Govt. Print. Off., 1941. xviii, 159 p. illus. ([U.S.] Work Projects Administration. Research monograph 24)   HV85.A36, no. 24
                               HV95.B8
Reprinted in New York by Da Capo Press in 1971 (HV95.B8 1971).

005

Carothers, Doris. Chronology of the Federal Emergency Relief Administration, May 12, 1933 to December 31, 1937. 163 p. ([U.S.] Works Progress Administration. Research monograph 6)   HV85.A36 no. 6
                               HV85.C3
Reprinted in New York by Da Capo Press in 1971 (HV95.C34 1971).
"Catalogs and Indexes of Publications of Federal Emergency Relief Administration, Works Progress Administration, and National Youth Administration.": p. 119.

006

Chapin, F. Stuart, and Julius A. Jahn. Advantages of work relief over direct relief in maintaining morale in St. Paul in 1939. American journal of sociology, v. 46, July 1940: 13-22.   HMl.A7, v. 46
Bibliographic footnotes.

007

Gill, Corrington. Wasted manpower; the challenge of unemployment. New York, W. W. Norton [c1939] 312 p. illus.
                               HD5724.G5
"Selected References": p. 299-302.

008

"Having the time of my life": letters from a wanderer, 1930-1932. Compiled and edited by Harvey Sletton. North Dakota history, v. 46, spring 1979: 14-21. illus.
                               F631.N862, v. 46

009

Hopkins, Harry L. Employment in America. Vital speeches of the day, v. 3, Dec. 1, 1936: 103-107.   PN6121.V52, v. 3
Evaluates economic recovery to date, pointing to continued high unemployment, calling for cooperation from industry, and expressing faith in the eventual success of government programs.

010

Hopkins, Harry L. Spending to save; the complete story of relief. New York, W. W. Norton [c1936] 197 p.   HV91.H6

011

Huzar, Elias. Federal unemployment relief policies: the first decade. Journal of politics, v. 2, Aug. 1940: 321-335.
                               JA1.J6, v. 2

012

Huzar, Elias. Legislative control over administration: Congress and the W.P.A.

American political science review, v. 36, Feb. 1942: 51-67.   JA1.A6, v. 36

013
Loomis, John P. Reds and rackets in work relief. Saturday evening post, v. 209, June 5, 1937: 25, 97-98, 100-104. illus.
                    AP2.S22, v. 209
What began as simple, forthright work relief has expanded into an unwieldy organization of overpaid bureaucrats vulnerable to fraud, corruption, and leftist influences.

014
Macmahon, Arthur W., John D. Millett, and Gladys Ogden. The administration of federal work relief. Chicago, Published for the Committee on Public Administration of the Social Science Research Council by Public Administration Service, 1941. 407 p. (Committee on Public Administration. Social Science Research Council. Studies in administration, v. 12)   HD3887.M3
Bibliographic footnotes.

015
"No one has starved." Fortune, v. 6, Sept. 1932: 18-29, 80, 82, 84. illus. (part col.)
                    HF5001.F7, v. 6
Public admission of the extent of unemployment has been slow to come.
Appendix A: "This State Will Care for its Own": p. 84, 86, 88. Appendix B: Estimates of unemployment: p. 88.

016
Schlesinger, Arthur M., Sr. The New Deal in action, 1933-1939. New York, Macmillan Co., 1940. 77 p. illus., map.   E178.H7165
"Select Bibliography": p. 76-77.

017
Shall we return relief to the states? Vital speeches of the day, v. 5, May 1, 1939: 431-434.   PN6131.V52, v. 5
Delivered at American Forum of the Air, Station WOL, Washington, D.C., April 16, 1939.
Contents: There would be disadvantages, by James F. Byrnes.—The administration of relief has been a scandal, by Charles L. McNary.

018
The Sharing of responsibility for relief: a discussion. Public administration review, v. 1, spring 1941: 231-241.   JK1.P85, v. 1
Contents: Editorial introduction.—The case for state-local administration, by William J. Ellis.—The case for retaining the federal W.P.A., by William Hodson.

"Looking Back": Post-1943 Publications

019
Allswang, John M. The New Deal and American politics: a study in political change. New York, Wiley, c1978, 155 p. (Critical episodes in American politics)   JK261.A64
Bibliography: p. 139-147.

020
Bendiner, Robert. Just around the corner; a highly selective history of the thirties. New York, Harper & Row [1967] xiv, 268 p. illus.   E806.B46
His own recollections and impressions.

021
Billington, Monroe. The Alabama clergy and the New Deal. Alabama review, v. 32, July 1979: 214-225.   F321.A2535, v. 32
Bibliographic footnotes.

022
Bird, Caroline. The invisible scar. New York, D. McKay Co. [1966] xviii, 364 p.

HC106.3.B5

Describes the years of the Depression, a period of standstill when economic growth stopped and paralysis spread. The effect of these years of "lost time, lost hope, lost opportunities, monotony, envy, and bitterness" was felt long after the economic recovery engendered by World War II was well under way.

023
Bonnifield, Mathew Paul. The Dust Bowl: men, dirt, and depression. Albuquerque, University of New Mexico Press, c1979. 232 p. illus.

F595.B73

Bibliographic references included in "Notes" (p. 203-216). Bibliography: p. 217-228.

The theory that the Dust Bowl was created by the intense greed of land developers and the cynical attitude of farmers toward the soil must be reevaluated. "Ultimately the story of the heartland of the dust bowl is the chronicle of hardworking, stouthearted folks who withstood the onslaught of nature at its worst, while living through a devastating depression and facing government idealism."

024
Braeman, John, Robert H. Bremner, and David Brody, eds. The New Deal. Columbus, Ohio State University Press [1975] 2 v. (Modern America, no. 4)

E806.B72

Contents: v. 1. The national level.—v. 2. The state and local levels.

Includes bibliographic references.

A collection of essays by 24 authors analyzing various aspects of the New Deal.

025
Bremer, William W. Along the "American Way": the New Deal's work relief programs for the unemployed. Journal of American history, v. 62, Dec. 1975: 636-652.

E171.J87, v. 62

Bibliographic footnotes.

Analyzes contemporary evaluations of work-relief effectiveness pointing out that the WPA was unable to meet its announced goal of providing real work and removing the stigma of welfare for its employees. Making WPA employment attractive would have been in conflict with another announced goal—encouraging workers to return to private industry as fast as possible.

026
Charles, Searle F. Minister of relief; Harry Hopkins and the Depression. [Syracuse, N.Y.] Syracuse University Press, 1963. 286 p. illus.

HV28.H66C47

Bibliographic references included in "Notes" (p. 249-268). Bibliography: p. 269-275.

027
Conkin, Paul K. The New Deal. New York, Crowell [1967] 118 p. (Crowell American history series)

E806.C6

"A Note on New Deal Historiography": p. 107-112.

028
Cowley, Malcolm. The dream of the golden mountains: remembering the 1930s. New York, Viking Press, 1980. 328 p. illus.

PS3505.O956Z464 1980

029
Elder, Glen H. Children of the Great Depression: social change in life experience.

Chicago, University of Chicago Press, c1974. xxiii, 400 p.   HN80.O18E43
Bibliographic references included in "Notes" (p. 337-376). "Select Bibliography": p. 377-388.
Longitudinal observations of an Oakland California sample were made over a thirty year period from 1934 to 1964.

030
Goldstein, Harold M. Regional barriers in the utilization of federal aid: the Southeast in the 1930's. Quarterly review of economics and business, v. 7, summer 1967: 65-70. illus.   HC10.Q33, v. 7
Bibliographic footnotes.
"The areas with the lowest income and the greatest need received the least in per capita work relief funds." Negroes and farmers were particularly neglected in consideration for WPA programs.

031
Goldston, Robert C. The Great Depression; the United States in the thirties. Illustrated with photos. and drawings by Donald Carrick. Indianapolis, Bobbs-Merrill [1968] 218 p. illus.   HC106.3.G58

032
Gurko, Leo. The angry decade. New York, Harper Row, 1968, c1947. 306 p.
PS221.G85 1968
American authors of the thirties viewed in the context of their times.

033
Jones, Alfred H. The search for a usable American past in the New Deal era. American quarterly, v. 23, Dec. 1971: 710-724.
AP2.A3985, v. 23
Bibliographic footnotes.

The renewed interest in America that stimulated work on the WPA guides and historical surveys was part of a larger national trend aimed at rediscovering American roots and reaffirming a national identity and pride.

034
Keeran, Roger. The Communist Party and the auto workers unions. Bloomington, Indiana University Press, c1980. 340 p.
HD6515.A8K43

035
Killigrew, John W. The impact of the Great Depression on the army [1929–1936] New York, Garland Pub., 1979. ca. 450 p. in various paging. (Modern American history)   UA25.K47 1979
Reprint of the 1960 edition of the author's thesis, Indiana University (UA25.K47).

036
Kimberly, Charles M. The Depression in Maryland: the failure of voluntaryism. Maryland historical magazine, v. 70, summer 1975: 189-202.   F176.M18, v. 70
Bibliographic footnotes.

037
Kurzman, Paul A. Harry Hopkins and the New Deal. Foreword by Louis W. Koenig. Fair Lawn, N.J., R. E. Burdick [1974] 219 p.
HV28.H66K87
Bibliography: p. 205-214.

038
Linford, Alton A. Public work and fiscal policy in the United States. Social services review, v. 18, Sept. 1944: 295-317. illus.
HV1.S6, v. 18

039
Mishkin, Frederic S. The household balance sheet and the Great Depression. Journal of economic history, v. 38, Dec. 1978: 918-937.   HC10.J64, v. 38
    Bibliographic footnotes.
    "This paper focuses on changes in household balance sheets . . . as transmission mechanisms which were important in the decline of aggregrate demand."

040
Mitchell, Broadus. Depression decade; from New Era through New Deal, 1929-1941. New York, Rinehart [1947] xviii, 462 p. illus. (The Economic history of the United States, v. 9)   HC103.E25, v. 9
    "The Literature of the Subject": p. 408-435.

041
Patterson, James T. The New Deal and the states. American historical review, v. 73, Oct. 1967: 70-84.   E171.A57, v. 73

042
Pells, Richard H. Radical visions and American dreams; culture and social thought in the Depression years. New York, Harper & Row [1973] 424 p.   E169.1.P42 1973

043
Rauch, Basil. The history of the New Deal, 1933-1938. New York, Creative Age Press [1944] 368 p.   E806.R3
    "Reference Notes": p. 341-351.

044
Scharf, Lois. To work and wed: female employment, feminism, and the Great Depression. Westport, Conn., Greenwood Press, c1980. (Contributions in women's studies, no. 15)   HD6095.S3

045
Schuyler, Michael W. Drought and politics 1936: Kansas as a test case. Great Plains journal, v. 15, fall 1975: 2-27. illus.
                              F591.G76, v. 15

046
Terkel, Louis. Hard times; an oral history of the Great Depression [by] Studs Terkel. New York, Pantheon Books [1970] 462 p.
                              E806.T45

047
Trout, Charles H. Welfare in the New Deal era. Current history, v. 65, July 1973: 11-14, 39.   D410.C82, v. 65
    Bibliographic footnotes.
    Federal work relief programs were often mismanaged at the local level where they were subjected to intergovernmental stresses and the pull of political and ethnic rivalries.

048
Warren, Frank A. Liberals and Communism; the "red decade" revisited. Bloomington, Indiana University Press [1966] 276 p.   HX528.W37 1966
    Includes bibliographic references.
    A study of the nature and extent of Communist influence in the thirties by examination of liberal writings and periodicals of the period.

049
Wecter, Dixon. The age of the Great Depression, 1929-1941. New York, Macmillan Co., 1948. xiv, 434 p. illus. (A history of American life, v. 18)   E806.W43 1948
    "Critical Essay on Authorities": p. 317-342. "Additional Footnotes": p. 343-413.

050

Wilson, Edmund. The thirties: from notebooks and diaries of the period. Edited with an introduction by Leon Edel. New York, Farrar, Straus, and Giroux, c1980. xxxii, 753 p.   PS3545.I6245Z535 1980

051

Worster, Donald E. Dust Bowl: the southern plains in the 1930s. New York, Oxford University Press, 1979. 277 p.   F786.W87
Bibliographic references included in "Notes" (p. [244]-271).

This ecological blunder was "the inevitable outcome of a culture that deliberately, self-consciously, set itself that task of dominating and exploiting the land for all it was worth." The social values and practices that produced the Dust Bowl also produced the Depression, and the two failures are closely linked.

Nursery school lunch in Chinatown, San Francisco (top left), a canning project in Colorado (top right), and garden cultivation in Missouri (bottom).

II

The Many Faces of the WPA

Before 1935 the Roosevelt administration had begun asking Congress for emergency relief appropriations while planning a coordinated authority that would manage the proposed work relief programs. The Emergency Relief Act of 1935 which made four billion dollars available for work relief was approved by President Roosevelt in April. By executive order he then set up the paper organization of the as yet untried works program. There were to be three branches—the Division of Applications and Information, the Advisory Committee on Allotments, and the Works Progress Administration. The role of the last was to be one of coordinating the program's operation, monitoring reports from the field, and administering some small projects where needed.

In practice the new mechanism quickly generated paperwork, confusion, and conflicting policies and procedures. The WPA, now also under the direction of Harry Hopkins, followed the model set by the FERA to become the primary administrative organ of the works program. As local WPA offices were set up at the state level, the importance of central application and approval procedures diminished.

The WPA developed a program of work relief that was designed to help the white collar worker and the artist as well as manual laborers. Hopkins held the belief (often unfashionable) that a violinist who could not find employment with a symphony orchestra should not be forced to dig ditches as an alternative. Eventually WPA programs did provide employment in art, theater, music, writing, and historical research.

In the meantime, the WPA put to work not only construction workers, but seamstresses, statisticians, teachers, craftsmen, and an army of clerks. They were located in offices, schools, hospitals, museums, parks, and libraries and engaged in a wide variety of tasks. The pencil was indeed an apt symbol for much of the work of the WPA.

In 1939 Congress revised the funding structure of the WPA and a general reorganization was conducted. Sponsorship of projects was transferred to the local level and federal control was considerably reduced. The project name was changed to the Work Projects Administration. The theater project was terminated in a flurry of criticism and controversy. In 1942 when demands of war made work relief unnecessary, the WPA received its "honorable discharge" from President Roosevelt and was finished.

The following references were selected to explore the diversity of "WPA jobs" and to provide more information about the administration of WPA programs and the public criticism that was often aimed at the WPA. It should be noted that some of the authors were WPA officials and, not surprisingly, express a positive opinion of the program's achievements.

"At the time": Pre-1943 Publications

052

Adams, Grace K. The white collar chokes; three years of WPA professional work. Harpers magazine, v. 177, Oct. 1938: 474-484.   AP2.H3, v. 177

Too often it seems that the repetitious and artificial nature of WPA clerical tasks has made a mockery of the concept that useful work is preferable to the dole. However, employment at these jobs has become a way of life for many workers, especially young ones, who cling to the WPA for security.

053

Adams, Grace K. Workers on relief. New Haven, Yale University Press, 1939. 344 p. illus.　　　　　　　HD3885.A55

　Fictionalized description of the experiences of several workers who found a place in the WPA.

054

Adult education under the Works Progress Administration. School and society, v. 48, Nov. 26, 1938: 692-694.　　L11.S36, v. 48

055

Aikman, Duncan. The WPA racket in Pennsylvania. American mercury, v. 38, May 1936: 28-35.　　　　　　AP2.A37, v. 38

056

Alden, Judith. Help! Literary digest, v. 124, Sept. 11, 1937: 18-20. illus.

　　　　　　　　　　AP2.L58, v. 124

　The WPA Household Training Program provides eight weeks of training in such chores as cooking, laundry, and bedmaking for workers who can then find positions as domestic helpers.

O57

Amidon, Beulah. WPA—wages and workers. Survey graphic, v. 24, Oct. 1935: 493-497, 504-505. illus.　　　　　HVl.S82, v. 24

　Because they are not paid union rates on their WPA jobs, skilled workers in the building trades have been striking in protest. Unfamiliar paycheck schedules, paperwork delays, and long lines are also WPA problems felt by needy workers.

058

Archibald, Raymond C. New York mathematics tables project. Science, new ser., v. 96, Sept. 25, 1942: 294-296.

　　　　　　　　　　Q1.S35, n.s., v. 96

　Two shifts of workers are kept busy calculating and publishing data to meet the needs of army and navy technicians and to fill approved requests of individual scientists.

059

Asch, Nathan. WPA adult education. American federationist, v. 45, Apr. 1938: 386-390.　　　　　　HD8055.A5A2, v. 45

060

Askew, Sarah B. WPA in New Jersey. Wilson library bulletin, v. 14, May 1940: 634-637. illus.　　　　　　Z1217.W75, v. 14

　WPA assistance has made extended public library service possible.

061

Bachart, Donald. I build a highway; why WPA worker No. 83202, Project No. 16523 K has every right to lean on his pick. North American review, v. 247, summer 1939: 241-250.　　　　　　AP2.N7, v. 247

　A writer by trade, the author describes his experiences in WPA road repair work in Ohio and analyzes questions frequently raised about work relief.

062

Binkley, Robert C. The cultural program of the W.P.A. Harvard educational review, v. 9, Mar. 1939: 156-174.　　L11.H3, v. 9

　An introduction to the problem of finding useful employment for "needy clericals" by one of the "idea men" who provided stimulation to project planning. His proposals included work in public records, library resources, school materials, and imprint inventories.

063

Blinn, Harold E. WPA newspaper clipping and indexing service. Pacific historical review, v. 6, Sept. 1937: 284-287.

F851.P18, v. 6

A project to collect newspaper material relating to the historical development of the Pacific Northwest. Clipped items are mounted separately, dated, and filed in boxes by subject; indexed items are noted on 3 x 5 cards from which subject indexes can be compiled for individual newspapers.

064

Bonsteel, Ruth M. A recreation-occupational-therapy project at a state hospital under W.P.A. auspices. Mental hygiene, v. 24, Oct. 1940: 552-565.   RA790.A1M5, v. 24

065

Borowski, Anthony J. WPA workers and trainees in the hospital. American journal of nursing, v. 41, Sept. 1941: 1023-1025.

RT1.A5, v. 41

66

Bristol, Margaret C. Personal reactions of assignees to W.P.A. in Chicago. Social service review, v. 12, Mar. 1938: 69-100.

HV1.S6, v. 12

Survey results with transcripts of some responses.

067

Burns, Arthur E., and Peyton Kerr. Recent changes in work-relief wage policy. American economic review, v. 31, Mar. 1941: 56-66.   HB1.E26, v. 31

Explanation of hourly wage schedules for WPA employees.

068

Cameron, Donald. Research projects aid schools and scholars. American scholar, v. 8, spring 1939: 248-250.

AP2.A4572, v. 8

WPA support is making university sponsored research possible in many fields including agriculture, engineering, commerce, and the sciences.

069

Campbell, Doak S., Frederick H. Bair, and Oswald L. Harvey. Educational activities of the Works Progress Administration. Prepared for the Advisory Committee on Education. Washington, U.S. Govt. Print. Off., 1939. xiv, 185 p. illus. ([U.S.] Advisory Committee on Education. Staff study no. 14)   L111.A93 no. 14

LA210.C3

"Publications of the Committee": p. 185.

070

Carmody, John M. The Federal Works Agency and public health. American journal of public health, v. 30, Aug. 1940: 887-894.   RA421.A41, v. 30

Summary of work carried out under all emergency relief programs, including WPA.

071

Carroll, Gordon. How the WPA buys votes. American mercury, v. 42, Oct. 1937: 194-213.   AP2.A37, v. 42

Charges that the WPA conceals its questionable practices and expenditures of "easy money" by attacking its critics with massive propaganda barrages manufactured by federal writers. The WPA's educational program promotes collectivism and anticapitalistic feelings, thereby paving the road to revolution.

072
Centralized gardening and canning for school lunches. Education for victory, v. 1, May 15, 1942: 27.   L11.E274, v. 1

073
Chimene, Eugene O. Neighbors lend a hand; a project in home hygiene. Hygeia, v. 15, Mar. 1937: 256-259, 286-288. illus.
                                    RA421.T6, v. 15
  Women from relief rolls were taught to be community workers who could go into neighborhoods like their own and provide advice and training on child care, sickbed nursing, nutrition, needs of the elderly, prenatal examinations, and cleanliness.

074
Cline, Dorothy I. Training for recreation; an account of the in-service training program, Division of Recreation, Works Progress Administration, October 1935-October 1937. [Chicago, University of Chicago Press] 1939. 130 p. illus.   GV53.C5
  Bibliographies: p. 121-130.

075
Contributions of the WPA to education. American teacher, v. 24, Apr. 1940: 7-21. illus.   L11.A85, v. 24
  Several short essays on various aspects of WPA educational work.

076
Coyle, David C. The WPA—loafers or workers? Forum and century, v. 101, Mar. 1939: 170-174.   AP2.F8, v. 101
  In most cases reports of WPA abuses could not be substantiated.

077
Dow, Edward F. Biggest boondoggle? South Atlantic quarterly, v. 38, July 1939: 316-331.   AP2.S75, v. 38
  A St. Louis project to build a card index of names in the 1900 census encountered many problems but found some solutions and ultimately provided a valuable service for people seeking proof of birthdate and other records.

078
Employment under the WPA, 1939. In U.S. Bureau of Labor Statistics. Monthly labor review, v. 51, Sept. 1940: 586-588.
                                    HD8051.A78, v. 51
  Presents tables of data from the WPA's progress report for 1939 showing the number of persons employed on various kinds of projects.

079
Five years' operation of the WPA. In U.S. Bureau of Labor Statistics. Monthly labor review, v. 52, Mar. 1941: 601-608.
                                    HD8051.A78, v. 52
  Includes statistical reports based on WPA estimates of work completed.

080
Fraenkel, Marta. Housekeeping service for chronic patients; an analysis of a service for the chronically sick and the infirm aged, operated by the Work Projects Administration. [New York] Welfare Council of New York City, 1942. xiv, 143 p. illus.
                                    RT61.F7
  "Bibliographical Notes": p. 142-143. Bibliographic footnotes.

081
Frazier, Corrine R. WPA serves the blind: an account of one set of projects which certainly cannot arouse controversy.

Commonweal, v. 30, Aug. 11, 1939: 371-372.   AP2.C6897, v. 30

082
Frazier, Corinne R. Why pay the fiddler? Parents' magazine, v. 12, Feb. 1937: 20-21, 71-74.   HQ768.P33, v. 12
    The public is getting its money's worth from WPA recreational projects, for they keep young people constructively occupied and out of trouble.

083
Gill, Corrington. W.P.A. Current history, v. 48, Jan. 1938: 36-42. illus.
                     D410.C8, v. 48
    Explains the "vital facts" of the WPA operation that one must understand before attempting to assess the merits or shortcomings of the program.

084
How can the work relief program be improved? A critical analysis of 7,737 surveys of WPA projects and methods. American city, v. 54, June 1939: 76-77, 108.
                     HT101.A5, v. 54

085
Hogan, Willard N. The WPA research and records program. Harvard educational review, v. 13, Jan. 1943: 52-62.
                     L11.H3, v. 13

086
Howard, Donald S. The WPA and federal relief policy. New York, Russell Sage Foundation, 1943. 879 p. illus.
                     HV95.H6 1943
    Bibliographic footnotes.

087
Judd, Maurice. Federal work program for better schools. School and society, v. 45, Mar. 20, 1937: 410-414. tables.
                     L11.S36, v. 45
    Notes on the construction, repair, or improvement of educational buildings. In many instances rural communities had no school until the WPA built one.

088
Kerr, Florence. Educational aids to handicapped children. School and society, v. 51, May 18, 1940: 642-646.   L11.S36, v. 51
    WPA teachers stress education, recreation, and vocational training.

089
Kerr, Florence. The WPA school lunch. Hygeia, v. 18, Dec. 1940: 1074-1076, 1083, 1096. illus.   RA421.T6, v. 18
    The WPA contribution to the school lunch program for needy children is primarily the labor provided to prepare and serve the meals. Food may come from community groups, WPA gardens and canneries, or the Surplus Marketing Administration.

090
Langdon, Grace, and Isabel J. Robinson. Nursery schools plus. School life, v. 26, Nov. 1940: 48-51. illus.   L11.S445, v. 26
    Pre-school-age children from low income families have been given nursery school opportunities along with coordinated training for their parents. The Family Life Education program of the WPA has also made parent education and homemaking training available to other interested adults.

091
Martin, Robert E. Wall around hell; how science is fighting the world's biggest fire in

Ohio. Popular science monthly, v. 132, June 1938: 34-35, 118. illus.

AP2.P8, v. 132

A coal mine fire that has burned for over fifty years is being subdued by WPA workers.

092

Millett, John D. The Works Progress Administration in New York City. Chicago, Published for the Committee on Public Administration of the Social Science Research Council by Public Administration Service, 1938. 228 p. illus. (Committee on Public Administration. Social Science Research Council. Studies in Administration, v. 2)   HD4606.N5M5 1938

093

Monaghan, James. A new source of information for historians. In Illinois State Historical Society. Journal, v. 30, July 1937: 163-170.   F536.I18, v. 30

A Chicago project that would create subject indexes for more than 800 foreign language periodicals and newspapers published in twenty languages in that city since 1871.

094

Myer, Elizabeth G. Rhode Island's state-wide library project. Wilson library bulletin, v. 16, May 1942: 755-757.

Z1217.W75, v. 16

095

Negroes under WPA, 1939. In U.S. Bureau of Labor Statistics. Monthly labor review, v. 50, Mar. 1940: 636-638.

HD8051.A78, v. 50

096

103 union presidents meet to urge Congress to change WPA wage-hour rates. American federationist, v. 46, Aug. 1939: 833-837.   HD8055.A5A42, v. 46

Remarks by President Green of the American Federation of Labor outlining the union's relationship to the WPA and its opinion of the new wage structure.

097

Perkins, John S. Extent and nature of the federal WPA educational program. School and society, v. 45, Jan. 23, 1937: 134-136. tables.   L11.S36, v. 45

WPA educational activities have been composed in large measure of general adult studies, vocational training, and literacy courses. Nursery schools and correspondence courses are popular too.

098

Russell, W. Duncan. "Never too old to play." Recreation, v. 31, Sept. 1937: 373-375, 396.   GV421.R5, v. 31

In Boston the adult recreation program is geared to the needs and interests of local neighborhoods.

099

Sinclair, Jo. I was on relief. Harpers magazine, v. 184, Jan. 1942: 159-163.

AP2.H3, v. 184

Expresses the doubts and fears experienced by the worker who moves to private industry after five years on WPA projects.

100

Von Struve, A. W. Educational program of the Works Progress Administration in New York. School and society, v. 48, Nov. 5, 1938: 594-596   L11.S36, v. 48

101

Von Struve, A. W. Data on foraminifera collected by the Works Progress Administration. Science, new ser., v. 86, Oct. 22, 1937: 374-375.   Q1.S35, n.s., v. 86

Through identification of the tiny fossilized remains of these microscopic, single-celled animals found in the rock layers making up the outer crust of the earth, an estimate can be made of the type of rock and soil to be encountered in drilling or excavating operations.

102

Von Struve, A. W. Two WPA projects of historical interest. Southwestern historical quarterly, v. 42, Oct. 1938: 117-121.
                                        F381.T45, v. 42

New Orleans' historic old Cabildo is being restored, while the Osages dedicate an Indian-owned museum.

103

The WPA and public health. American federationist, v. 45, June 1938: 600-603.
                                HD8055.A5A2, v. 45

104

Wheeler, Burton K. W.P.A. and politics; abuses in government aid. Vital speeches of the day, v. 4, Sept. 1, 1938: 681-683.
                                    PN6121.V52, v. 4

105

White-collar work under the W.P.A. In U.S. Bureau of Labor Statistics. Monthly labor review, v. 45, Dec. 1937: 1364-1369.
                                    HD8051.A78, v. 45

106

Wilder, Grace. Puppetry in a new age. Recreation, v. 30, July 1936: 207-208, 227-228.
                                        GV421.R5, v. 30

A New York recreation project brought enjoyment to the young people who built the puppets and planned the shows and to the many others who viewed the performances in parks and playgrounds.

107

Woodward, Ellen S. 80,000,000 meals! [WPA school lunch program] Hygeia, v. 15, Nov. 1937: 1015-1017. illus.
                                        RA421.T6, v. 15

108

Woodward, Ellen S. The WPA and nursing. American journal of nursing, v. 37, Sept. 1937: 994-997.   RT1.A5, v. 37

A note in the June 1938 issue (p. 733) contains a statistical correction from the author regarding the number of registered nurses employed on WPA health projects.

109

Woodward, Ellen S. WPA library projects. Wilson library bulletin, v. 12, Apr. 1938: 518-520. illus.   Z1217.W75, v. 12

Library extension projects have started new reading rooms and established mobile library service, bringing books into rural areas by truck, horseback, and bookmobile.

110

Wright, Roscoe. WPA: a community appraisal. Current history, v. 49, Feb. 1939: 42-44. illus.   D410.C8, v. 49

Survey data from hundreds of individual communities indicate general satisfaction with WPA accomplishments.

"Looking Back": Post-1943 Publications

111

Blumberg, Barbara. The New Deal and the unemployed: the view from New York City.

Lewisburg [Pa.] Bucknell University Press, c1979. 332 p. illus. HD4606.N5B58 1979
Includes bibliographic references. "Selected Bibliography": p. 307-317.
Describes many aspects of WPA work in the city, with mention also of politics and legislation.

112
Burran, James A. The WPA in Nashville, 1935-1943. Tennessee historical quarterly, v. 34, fall 1975: 293-306.
F431.T285, v. 34
Bibliographic footnotes.

113
Clement, Priscilla F. The Works Progress Administration in Pennsylvania, 1935 to 1940. Pennsylvania magazine of history and biography, v. 95, Apr. 1971: 244-260.
F146.P65, v. 95
Bibliographic footnotes.

114
Erickson, Herman. WPA strike and trials of 1939. Minnesota history, v. 42, summer 1971: 203-214. illus.   F601.M72, v. 42
In Minneapolis and St. Paul protest followed passage of the 1939 Emergency Relief Appropriation Act which reduced hourly wages and increased the hours of work required on WPA jobs there.

115
Evans, Timothy K. "This certainly is relief.": Matthew S. Murray and Missouri politics during the Depression. In Missouri Historical Society, St. Louis, Bulletin, v. 28, July 1972: 219-233.   F461.M6226, v. 28
As director of Public Works for Kansas City and Missouri State Administrator for the WPA, Murray used his power to create a "finely oiled political machine" feeding votes to candidates endorsed by Boss Tom Pendergast.

116
Harney, Andy L. WPA handicrafts rediscovered. Historic preservation, v. 25, July 1973: 10-15. illus.   E151.H5, v. 25
The handicraft projects were not sponsored by the arts program, but grew out of local efforts such as the sewing projects. Work from many states is described, particularly Timberline Lodge in Oregon which was built, furnished, and decorated by WPA technicians and craft workers.

117
Leupold, Robert J. The Kentucky WPA: relief and politics, May-November 1935. Filson Club historical quarterly, v. 49, Apr. 1975: 152-168.   F446.F484, v. 49
Bibliographic footnotes.

118
Marcello, Ronald E. The selection of North Carolina's WPA chief, 1935: a dispute over political patronage. North Carolina historical review, v. 52, Jan. 1975: 59-76. ports.
F251.N892, v. 52

119
Rader, Frank J. Work relief and national defense: some notes on WPA in Alaska. Alaska journal, v. 6, winter 1976: 54-59. illus.   F901.A342, v. 6

120
Stanford, Edward B. Library extension under the WPA; an appraisal of an experiment in federal aid. Chicago, University of Chicago Press [1944] 284 p. illus.
Z731.S8 1944a

Thesis (Ph.D.)—University of Chicago, 1942

Published also without thesis note in the series University of Chicago studies in library science.

Bibliography: p. 269-284.

Bibliography includes references to many short articles on library extension services, library work relief, and state-wide library projects that might be passed over in a less comprehensive list. Also included are references to project manuals, reports, and newspapers.

121

Studies in creative partnership: federal aid to public libraries during the New Deal. Edited by Daniel F. Ring. Metuchen, N.J., Scarecrow Press, 1980. 145 p. illus.

Z731.S895

Contents: "Almost a boon . . .": federal relief programs and the Enoch Pratt Free Library, 1933-1943, by John Calvin Colson.—The Cleveland Public Library and the W.P.A.: a study in creative partnership, by Daniel F. Ring.—The Chicago Public Library W.P.A. Omnibus Project, by Alex Ladenson.—The W.P.A. and the New York Public Library, by Margot Karp and Rhoda Garoogian.—The New Deal work projects at the Milwaukee Public Library, by Daniel F. Ring.—The Minneapolis Public Library and the W.P.A. experience: collaboration for community need, by John Franklin White.—The W.P.A. and the San Francisco Public Library, by Fay M. Blake.—Notes on contributors.—Index.

122

Valentine, Jerry W. The WPA and Louisiana education. Louisiana history, v. 13, fall 1972: 391-395.   F336.J68, v. 30

Bibliographic footnotes. "Selected Footnotes": p. 394-395.

123

Whatley, Larry. The Works Progress Administration in Mississippi. Journal of Mississippi history, v. 30, Feb. 1968: 35-50.

F336.J68, v. 30

Bibliographic footnotes.

Music copyists in Philadelphia

III

Federal One: The Arts Projects Considered Together

It seems likely that WPA planners did not originally intend to sponsor an arts program at the national level. While they were sympathetic to the needs of unemployed artists, they tended to visualize work relief as being administered by states and regions. However, the appropriation of 1935 contained money earmarked for assistance to professional people employed on federally sponsored projects. To meet this requirement, the WPA created Federal Project Number One, which set up programs in art, music, theater, and writing—each with a national director.

This arrangement, not surprisingly, created conflict and hard feelings. Work relief for artists, actors, and musicians was not popular with local state administrators of the WPA who had difficulty visualizing painting or singing as work, a view that was generally shared by the press and some congressmen. But, asserted the state officials, if there were to be such programs, then state officials should manage them. Thus, the artists and professors that the national directors wanted to appoint to organize local art projects often received the cold shoulder and little cooperation when they arrived in the field.

Nevertheless, Federal One began to move. By late summer 1935 four national directors had been chosen: for art, Holger Cahill, for music, Nikolai Sokoloff, for theater, Hallie Flanagan, and for the writers' project, Henry Alsberg. Each was talented and enthusiastic; their devotion was reflected in the eventual success of many of their projects. Almost unwittingly the New Deal had launched the most extensive program of government support for the arts that the nation had ever seen.

The following references are concerned with all the arts programs. Individual programs will be treated separately in later sections.

124
Billington, Ray A. Government and the arts: the W.P.A. experience. American quarterly, v. 13, winter 1961: 466-479.
                    AP2.A3985, v. 13
    Describes his experiences as part-time director of the writers' project in Massachusetts and analyzes some of the problems that touched all of the arts projects. These included the acceptance of mediocrity and its counterpart, the stifling of genius, the tendency to base decisions on political considerations, the desire of some employees to use the arts projects for propaganda purposes, and the constant threat of censorship.

125
Lindeman, Eduard C. Farewell to Bohemia. Survey graphic, v. 26, Apr. 1937: 207-211. illus.   HV1.S82, v. 26
    Federal One has brought American artists out of their exclusive community and into touch with the common people. They are "painting American 'stuff' on the walls of American buildings, acting plays before audiences who can pay only 50 cents for a theater seat, [and] furnishing music to farmers and workers in school buildings paid for out of public taxation."

126
McDonald, William F. Federal relief administration and the arts; the origins and administrative history of the arts projects of the Works Progress Administration. [Columbus] Ohio State University Press [1969] xiv, 869 p.   NX735.M3
    Includes bibliographic references.

WILLING HANDS
THAT HAVE BEEN PUT TO WORK
FOR THE NATION
AT THE KIND OF WORK
• THEY ARE TRAINED TO DO.

Illustration for an information booklet showing a WPA orchestra

Extensive analysis of five projects of Federal One. The Historical Records Survey, originally part of the Writers' Project, was the fifth.

127
Mathews, Jane D. Arts and the people: the New Deal quest for a cultural democracy. Journal of American history, v. 62, Sept. 1975: 316-339.   E171.J87, v. 62
    Bibliographic footnotes.
    The national government, as a sponsor of culture, was thought to be a suitable agent to introduce fine painting, music, and drama into the lives of average Americans with the hope that the arts might become "both expressive of the spirit of a nation and accessible to its people."

128
Meltzer, Milton. Violins and shovels: the WPA arts projects. New York, Delacorte Press [1976] 160 p.   NX735.M44
    Bibliography: p. [150]-153.

129
Overmyer, Grace. Government and the arts. New York, W. W. Norton [1939] 338 p.
                      N8725.O8
    Bibliography: p. 325-327.
    "Our First Art Unit: The Section of Painting and Sculpture": p. 95-108. "Our Little Renaissance: The Four Arts Projects": p. 109-137.

130
Unemployed arts. Fortune, v. 15, May 1937: 108-117, 168, 171-172. illus. (part col.)
                      HF5001.F7, v. 15
    Analysis of the four WPA cultural projects—art, music, theater, writers—noting the diversity of tasks performed and the millions of people whose lives have been touched in one way or another by these artistic efforts.

131
Warren-Findley, Jannelle J. Culture and the New Deal [review essay] American studies, v. 17, spring 1976: 81-82.
                      E169.1.A486, v. 17

A mural painter on the job

IV

The Art of the Thirties and the Federal Art Project

As early as 1933 the Treasury Department (at that time the custodial agent for federal buildings) had administered the Public Works of Art Project under the auspices of Harry Hopkins' Civil Works Administration. The PWAP was terminated in 1934, but other Treasury programs for artistic improvement of public buildings were developed and continued under the direction of Edward Bruce, a talented artist who had originally been hired as a monetary expert on silver. The Section of Painting and Sculpture (later the Section of Fine Art) ran from 1934 to 1943, financed primarily by appropriations for federal buildings. The Section did not have a poverty test and selected artists by competence and competition. The Treasury Relief Art Program (1935-1939) was funded by the WPA; its focus was the decoration of federal buildings whose construction budgets had not included money for murals or sculpture. Many of the murals popularly attributed to the WPA's art project were in fact Treasury works.

Holger Cahill was named director of the Federal Art Project. He approached his task of creating work relief for artists with the conviction that art and those who create it must be integral parts of society, taking as well as giving inspiration. WPA artists worked on murals, easel works, and sculpture. An impressive exhibit of their products was presented at the 1940 New York World's Fair, where it was viewed by over two million people.

Because the Federal Art Project sought to find a place for every starving artist, even those whose talents were marginal, it sponsored production in all the major visual art fields and ran extensive educational programs. Some FAP employees worked in poster print shops, some engaged in photography,

some handcrafted items, and others helped to establish community art centers where free lessons and exhibitions were given. Painters were sent to museums to sketch examples of American folk art, from Shaker chairs to weathervanes. Their drawings, done with almost photographic accuracy, were designated the Index of American Design.

Predictably there were critics in abundance. Anti-New Dealers called the project boondoggling; anti-intellectuals ridiculed the notion that painting could be work; politicians found suspicious Communist influences everywhere. Still the project moved bravely ahead from 1935 through 1938, bringing aid and stimulation to millions, until criticism finally forced restructuring of the WPA in 1939. At that time Federal One was abolished and control of the cultural projects was transferred to the states, where many artists lost their jobs because of budget restrictions and new rules. In an attempt to recover some costs, sales of WPA art were held during two Art Weeks in 1940 and 1941. Increasing threats of war and the demands of defense turned the efforts of remaining artists to war work, such as creating posters and designing training materials.

"At the Time": Pre-1943 Publications

132
Art in federal buildings, an illustrated record of the Treasury Department's new program in painting and sculpture. v. 1. Mural designs, 1934-1936. Washington, D.C., Art in Federal Buildings Inc., 1936. xvi, 309 p. illus.   N6512.A7
   Text by Edward Bruce and Forbes Watson.
   No more published?
   "Biographical Notes": p. 291-309.

133

Biddle, George. Art under five years of federal patronage. American scholar, v. 9, summer 1940: 327-338.

AP2.A4572, v. 9

Criticizes the administrative location of federal art projects, suggesting that the Section of Fine Arts should not be managed by the bureaucracy of the Public Buildings Administration but might be joined to the WPA art project to form an integrated federal art program.

134

Cahill, Holger. American art today and in the world of tomorrow: national panorama of the WPA projects. Art news, v. 38, annual supplement, May 25, 1940: 49-50. illus.   N1.A6, v. 38

Description of the WPA exhibit at the 1939 World's Fair.

135

Federal Art Project. Art as a function of government, a survey. [New York] Supervisors Association of the WPA Federal Art Project, 1937. 32 p.   N8725.F4 1937

Includes a brief description of the many divisions of the Federal Art Project.

136

New York (City). Museum of Modern Art. New horizons in American art; with an introduction by Holger Cahill. New York, The Museum of Modern Art, 1936. 171 p. illus.   N5020.N44 1936

Reprinted in New York by Arno Press in 1969 (N6512.N436 1970).

"Exhibition of work done under the Federal Art Project of the Works Progress Administration . . . a documented survey of one year's activity"—foreword.

"Looking Back": Post-1943 Publications

137

Ajay, Abe. Working for the WPA. Art in America, v. 60, Sept./Oct. 1972: 70-75. illus. (part col.)   N1.A43, v. 60

Nostalgic recall of the kinship and enthusiasm shared by project artists.

138

Baigell, Matthew. The American scene: American painting of the 1930's. New York, Praeger [1974] 214 p. illus. (part col.) (American art & artists)

ND212.B28

Bibliography: p. 212.

139

Beckh, Erica. Government art in the Roosevelt era. Art journal, v. 20, fall 1960: 1-8   N8.A887, v. 20

An appraisal of the FAP and its predecessor, the Public Works of Art Project.

140

Bernstein, Joel H. The artist and the government: the P.W.A.P. In Challenges in American culture. Edited by Ray B. Browne, Larry N. Landrum [and] William K. Bottorff. Bowling Green, Ohio, Bowling Green University Press [1970] p. [69]-84.   E169.1.C43

141

Cahill, Holger. Artists in war and peace. Studio, v. 130, July 1945: 1-16. illus. (part col.)   N1.S9, v. 130

In their paintings WPA artists reflected their own localities and traditions—city, factory, mountain, or plain, piecing together from many perspectives the face of America.

A mural artist in New York City

142

Dieterich, Herbert R., and Jacqueline Petravage. New Deal art in Wyoming: some case studies. Annals of Wyoming, v. 45, spring 1973: 53-68.   F756.A67, v. 45

143

Harrison, Helen A. American art and the New Deal. Journal of American studies, v. 6, Dec. 1972: 289-296.   E151.J6, v. 6

144

Key, Donald. Milwaukee's art of the Depression era. Historical messenger, v. 31, summer 1975: 38-49. illus. F587.M6H5, v. 31

145

McCoy, Garnett, comp. Poverty, politics and artists, 1930-1945. Art in America, v. 53, Aug./Sept. 1965: 88-107. illus. (part col.)
                    N1.A43, v. 53
    Compiled from material contained in the collections of the Archives of American Art, the article includes passages from George Biddle's diary as well as color reproductions and many photographs.

146

McKinzie, Richard D. The New Deal for artists. [Princeton] Princeton University Press [1973] 203 p. illus.   N8838.M32
    Includes bibliographic references.

147

The New Deal art projects; an anthology of memoirs. Edited by Francis V. O'Connor. Washington, Smithsonian Institution, 1972. 339 p. illus.   N8838.N4
    Bibliography: p. 330-331.
    Contents: The New Deal's Treasury art program: a memoir, by Olin Dows.—A general view of the WPA Federal Art Project in New York city and state, by Audrey McMahon.—The New Deal mural projects, by Edward Laning.—The easel division of the WPA Federal Art Project, by Joseph Solman.—The New Deal sculpture projects, by Robert Cronbach.—The graphic arts division of the WPA Federal Art Project, by Jacob Kainen.—The Index of American Design of the WPA Federal Art Project by Lincoln Rothschild.—Artists' organizations of the Depression, by Lincoln Rothschild.—The American abstract artists and the WPA Federal Art Project, by Rosalind Bengelsdorf Browne.—The WPA Federal Art Project and the New York World's Fair, 1939-1940, by Olive Lyford Gavert.—A memoir of the New York City municipal art galleries, 1936-1939, by Marchal E. Landgren.—A dialogue, by Audrey McMahon, Marchal E. Landgren, Jacob Kainen, Olive Lyford Gavert, and Francis V. O'Connor.

148

O'Connor, Francis V., comp. Art for the millions; essays from the 1930s by artists and administrators of the WPA Federal Art Project. Greenwich, Conn., New York Graphic Society [1973] 317 p. illus.
                    N8838.O25
    "Selected Bibliography": p. 309.
    Collection of materials was begun in 1936 as the basis for a national progress report on WPA art programs. The diversity of projects undertaken is suggested by the organization of the essays—the fine arts, the practical arts, and art education.

149

O'Connor, Francis V. New Deal murals in New York. Artforum, v. 7, Nov. 1968: 41-49. illus.   N1.A814, v. 7

150

Purcell, Ralph. Government and art, a study of American experience. Washington, Public Affairs Press [1956] 129 p.
N6512.P8

Includes bibliographic references.
"New Stirrings: Federal Sponsorship and Assistance": p. 46-75.

151

A Sampler of New Deal murals. American heritage, v. 21, Oct. 1970: 45-57. illus. (part col.) E171.A43, v. 21

With a four-page foldout of Victor Arnautoff's *City Life* from Coit Tower in San Francisco.

152

Vitz, Robert C. Struggle and response: American artists and the Great Depression. New York history, v. 17, Jan. 1976: 80-98. illus. F116.N865, v. 17

153

Werner, Alfred. WPA and social realism. Art and artists, v. 10, Oct. 1975: 24-31. illus.
N1.A353, v. 10

THE INDEX OF AMERICAN DESIGN

154

Christensen, Erwin O. American popular art as recorded in the Index of American Design. Art in America, v. 35, July 1947: 199-208. illus. N1.A43, v. 35

155

Davidson, Marshall B. The WPA's amazing artistic record of American design. American heritage, v. 23, Feb. 1972: 65-80. illus. (part col.) E171.A43, v. 23

Additional color sketches also accompanied by Marshall B. Davidson's notes appear in "The Legacy of Craftsmen," in the April 1972 issue, p. 81-96.

156

Glassgold, C. Adolph. Color microfilm studies of the Index of American Design. Journal of documentary reproduction, v. 2, Sept. 1939: 214-217. Z265.J86, v. 2

157

Index of American Design: a portfolio. Fortune, v. 15, June 1937: 103-110. col. illus.
HF5001.F7, v. 15

Federal Writers' Project in Washington, D.C., 1937

V

Literature in the Depression: The Federal Writers' Project

Work relief programs for unemployed writers were slow to appear. When it became clear that the government was going to make jobs for artists, impoverished authors began to organize and to demonstrate in the streets demanding assistance. An early local assignment devised to fill the gap was in newspaper work. The task, which required investigation of facts followed by the writing of a feature or human nature story, foreshadowed the dominant work method that would be used by the writers' project—searching and describing.

When brought under the umbrella of Federal One, writers were officially recognized as artists eligible for government support. The first problem faced by the Federal Writers' Project and its national director, Henry G. Alsberg, was what shall we write? While authors might dream that government sponsorship would allow them the freedom to create true poetry, fiction, and drama without commercial constraints, Congress and the taxpayers did not share that vision.

The plan that was settled on was the compilation of travel guides to describe local history, major cities, and tours for each state. Such a project had the advantage of being locally adaptable and capable of employing large numbers of people. The original goal was the further distillation of regional material into one comprehensive American guidebook, but practical considerations dictated a separate book for each state.

The writers' project suffered from many of the problems that had dogged the other projects—incompetence (because of the need to hire any indigent self-termed writer), fears of censorship (the Massachusetts guide was severely criticized for including a section on the Sacco-Vanzetti trial), charges of Communist infiltration, and conflict between local and national WPA officials. A unique problem of the FWP was its low visibility. The public heard the music of federal musicians, saw federal players in performance, and watched federal murals appear on post office walls, but there was little general awareness of writers writing.

Project employees ranged from the professional to the marginal and included teachers, lawyers, doctors, clerks, and students. Alsberg sought experienced writers and editors to head each state's project and hoped enough qualified people could be found locally to train and supervise the "writers." Out into the states they went, collecting regional history and recording points of interest along the highways and in the cities. The editorial task of checking and coordinating the mass of reports that came back was huge. Introducing consistency into the publication of guides from different states and different editors was also difficult. Of necessity, the headquarters staff in Washington was large because of these editorial demands.

The first book completed was Idaho's, although its editor, Vardis Fisher, was engaged in feisty competition by the national office, which wanted the Washington, D.C., guide to appear first. Eventually a guide was published for each of the 48 states, Alaska, the District of Columbia, and Puerto Rico. There were also many local publications about cities and regions.

The published guides were generally well received by reviewers who noted some unevenness of style, but found the faults more than compensated for by the fascinating nuggets of local information that were turned up. Some observers noted a renaissance of interest in America. From the gloom of the early thirties, the writers' project led the nation to a reexamination of its heritage and a reaffirmation of its greatness.

While work on the guides was to be given priority, there were other projects, most related in some way to the writers' primary activity, exploration of the states. WPA writers also collected local folklore, anecdotes, and tales, studied local place-names and their origins, took life histories of long-time residents, sought information on resident ethnic groups, and interviewed former slaves to obtain a picture of life under slavery. They produced creative writing too— short stories and poems— many of them written after the 30-hour WPA work week was completed. An issue of *Poetry* (July 1938) was devoted to poems of the WPA. Another collection, *American Stuff; an Anthology of Prose and Verse by Members of the Federal Writers' Project,* was published in New York by Viking Press in 1937.

The demise of the writers' project paralleled that of the WPA. In 1939 support for the work was transferred to the local level. Increasingly the demands of the defense industry diminished the need for work relief. War-related writing projects were undertaken until the work of the WPA was terminated.

"At the Time": Pre-1943 Publications

158
Bolles, Blair. The Federal Writers' Project. Saturday review of literature, v. 18, July 9, 1938: 3-4, 18-19. illus.   Z1219.S25, v. 18

The guidebooks are notable for their wealth of material and abundance of little-known facts.

159
Botkin, Benjamin A. WPA and folklore research. Southern folklore quarterly, v. 3, Mar. 1939: 7-14.   GR1.S65, v. 3

Folklore collection crosses the many branches of Federal One and some of the other divisions of the WPA. Activity is now being coordinated by the Joint Committee on Folk Arts to avoid needless duplication of effort by those working with music, arts and crafts, drama, story-telling, leisure, education, and recreation.

160
Cantwell, Robert. America and the writers' project. New republic, v. 98, Apr. 26, 1939: 323-325.   AP2.N624, v. 98

Samples the interesting and unusual items of local history to be found in the guides.

161
Colby, Merle E. Presenting America to all Americans. Publishers' weekly, v. 139, May 3, 1941: 1828-1831. illus.

Z1219.P98, v. 139

Taken together the guide volumes make up an encyclopedia of contemporary America—"its legends, history, industry, geology, folklore, architecture, eminent men and women, social currents, [and] significant scenes."

162
Cowley, Malcolm. Poetry project. Poetry, v. 52, July 1938: 224-227.   PS301.P6, v. 52

The FWP has not been ideal for poets, for they have been set to writing guidebooks rather than poetry. However, they have had "food and lodging and in their leisure hours, they have been able to produce their poems."

163
Current-Garcia, Eugene. American panorama. Prairie schooner, v. 12, summer 1938: 79-90.   AP2.P85285, v. 12
Defends the writers' project, using *The New Orleans City Guide* as an example of the guidebooks' ability to capture local color and atmosphere.

164
Current-Garcia, Eugene. Writers in the "sticks." Prairie schooner, v. 12, winter 1938: 294-309.   AP2.P85285, v. 12
Biographical sketches of some of the project's state directors (Ulric R. Bell, Edwin Bjorkman, J. Frank Davis, Lyle Saxon, Ross Santee, Vardis Fisher, Harlan Hatcher, and J. Harris Gable), noting their backgrounds and qualifications.

165
DeVoto, Bernard. New England via W.P.A. Saturday review of literature, v. 18, May 14, 1938: 3-4, 14. illus.   Z1219.S25, v. 18
Detailed analysis of six state guides, pointing to weaknesses and irrelevancies in some of the essays, errors in some facts reported, the generally high quality of the tours described, and the intriguing array of local material unearthed.

166
DeVoto, Bernard. The writers' project. Harpers magazine, v. 184, Jan. 1942: 221-224.   AP2.H3, v. 184

167
Distributing the WPA guides. Publishers' weekly, v. 137, May 11, 1940: 1836-1839.   Z1219.P98, v. 137

168
Douglass, Eri. The Federal Writers' Project in Mississippi. Journal of Mississippi history, v. 1, Apr. 1939: 71-76.   F336.J68, v. 1

169
Glicksberg, Charles I. The Federal Writers' Project. South Atlantic quarterly, v. 37, Apr. 1938: 158-169.   AP2.S75, v. 37
Despite a barrage of public criticism from without and haggling within, the FWP has been able to give its writers a renewed sense of their own worth and represents a pioneering step in government support for the arts.

170
Gutheim, Frederick. America in guide books. Saturday review of literature, v. 24, June 14, 1941: 3-5, 15. illus.   Z1219.S25, v. 24

171
Hatcher, Harlan. The historical opportunities offered through the writers' project. Ohio archaeological and historical quarterly, v. 47, July 1938: 246-247.   F486.O51, v. 47
Describes the staff of the Ohio unit and some of its projects.

172
Johns, Orrick. Time of our lives; the story of my father and myself. New York, Stackpole Sons, [1937] 353 p. ports.   PS3519.O135Z5
Closes with an account of his experiences as director of the writers' project in New York City (p. 342-350).

173
Kazin, Alfred. The literature of crisis (1930-1940). In his On native grounds; an inter-

pretation of modern American prose literature. New York, Reynal & Hitchcock [1941] p. 363-518.   PS379.K3

WPA guides contributed significantly to a new experience of national self-discovery as scores of writers sought out the news of each road and byway. This "drive toward national inventory which began by reporting the ravages of the depression and ended by reporting on the national inheritance" altered the course of American literature for decades to come.

174

Kellock, Katharine. The WPA writers; portraitists of the United States. American scholar, v. 9, autumn 1940: 473-482.
                    AP2.A4572, v. 9

Examines the background of the project, noting the literary deficiencies of many of the employees, some of whom improved with diligent practice. Work on the state guides which required close scrutiny of many phases of American life seemed to rekindle patriotism among these disheartened writers.

175

Kreymborg, Alfred. Bread and poetry. Poetry, v. 52, July 1938: 220-223.
                    PS301.P6, v. 52

176

[Straus, Harold] Work of the Federal Writers' Project of WPA. Publishers' weekly, v. 135, Mar. 18, 1939: 1130-1135. illus.
                    Z1219.P98, v. 135

177

Touhey, Eleanor. The American Baedekers. Library journal, v. 66, Apr. 15, 1941: 339-341.   Z671.L7, v. 66

An evaluation of the American Guide Series including some comments from literary critics.

178

Ulrich, Mabel S. Salvaging culture for the WPA. Harpers magazine, v. 178, May 1939: 653-664.   AP2.H3, v. 178

A firsthand account of the responsibilities of a state director, who had to cope with the demands of the federal editors while finding jobs for "writers" who couldn't write. Ulrich analyzes the deterioration over time of WPA programs due to changes in the psychic makeup of relief employees, the disruption of Communist agitation, and the loss of sympathetic support at the national level.

"Looking Back": Post-1943 Publications

179

Aaron, Daniel. Writers on the left. New York, Harcourt, Brace & World [1961] xvi, 460 p. (Communism in American life)
                    PS228.C6A2

Bibliographic references included in "Notes" (p. 401-448).

Analysis of American writers who leaned toward Communist ideology during the period from 1912 to the early 1940's.

180

Birdsall, Esther K. The FWP and the popular press. In Challenges in American Culture. Edited by Ray B. Browne, Larry N. Landrum [and] William K. Bottorff. Bowling Green, Ohio, Bowling Green University Popular Press [1970] p. [101]-110.
                    E169.1.C43

Selections from contemporary reviews

of the guidebooks and other publications of the writers' project.

181

Blassingame, John W. Using the testimony of ex-slaves: approaches and problems. Journal of southern history, v. 41, Nov. 1975: 473-492.   F206.J68, v. 41

Notes many sources of bias in gathering material and preparing the reports.

182

Botkin, Benjamin A. Living lore on the New York City writers' project. New York folklore quarterly, v. 2, Nov. 1946: 252-263.
GR1.N473, v. 2

Descriptions of how the material was collected with some samples.

183

Botkin, Benjamin A. We called it "living lore." New York folklore quarterly, v. 14, fall 1958: 189-201.   GR1.N473, v. 14

Describes the "imaginative approach to folk life, thought, and fantasy" considered desirable by editors on the folklore projects.

184

Clayton, Ronnie W. Federal Writers' Project for blacks in Louisiana. Louisiana history, v. 19, summer 1978: 327-335.
F366.L6238, v. 19

Black researchers reached conclusions about the nature of slavery in Louisiana that were considerably different from those of the white writers.

185

Cowley, Malcolm. Federal Writers' Project. New republic, v. 167, Oct. 21, 1972: 23-26.   AP2.N624

In a review of Jerre Mangione's *The Dream and the Deal,* Cowley offers his own conclusions about the nature of the writers' program.

186

Cowley, Malcolm. A remembrance of the red romance. Esquire, v. 61, Mar. 1964: 124-128, 130; Apr.: 78-79, 81. illus.
AP2.E845, v. 61

Concerning that "grimly glamorous period" when many writers in America seemed to be drawn to Communism.

187

Culbert, David H. The infinite variety of mass experience: the Great Depression, W.P.A. interviews, and student family history projects. Louisiana history, v. 19, winter 1978: 43-63. illus.   F366.L6238, v. 19

Notes similarities between the techniques used in the WPA studies and the procedures used by students in gathering family histories.

188

Farran, Don. The federals in Iowa: a Hawkeye guidebook in the making. Annals of Iowa, 3d ser., v. 41, winter 1973: 1190-1196.   F616.A6, 3d s., v. 41

189

Fox, Daniel M. The achievement of the Federal Writers' Project. American quarterly, v. 13, spring 1961: 3-19.
AP2.A3985, v. 13

A review of the American Guide Series which suggests that the historical sections tend to be weak, indicating an impatience with tradition on the part of the writers.

190

Hirsch, Jerrold, and Tom E. Terrill. Conceptualization and implementation: some thoughts on reading the Federal Writers' Project southern life histories. Southern studies: an interdisciplinary journal of the South, v. 18, fall 1979: 351-362.

Not currently available at LC.

Includes bibliographic references.

Notes on the process of collecting and selecting interviews and the place of interviewer bias.

191
Lawrence, Kenan B. Oral history of slavery, by Ken Lawrence. Southern exposure, v. 1, winter 1974: 84-86. illus.

F206.S643, v. 1

192
Mangione, Jerre G. The dream and the deal; the Federal Writers' Project, 1935-1943. Boston, Little, Brown [1972] xvi, 416 p. illus. E175.4.W9M3 MRR Ref Desk

"Selected Publications of the WPA Federal Writers' Project and the Writers' Program": p. 375-396.

Anecdotal accounts of many of the people and projects of the FWP as seen from the national office in Washington, D.C., where Mangione was employed.

193
The 1930's, a symposium (with poems, a story, and reviews). [Compiled by Erling Larson] Carleton miscellany, v. 6, winter 1965: 6-113. AS30.C34, v. 6

Reminiscences about life and literature during the Depression by Dorothy Allen, Russell Ames, Benjamin Appel, James T. Farrell, Benjamin A. Botkin, Edwin Georgrichard Bruell, Jack Conroy, Malcolm Cowley, David Cornel DeJong, August Derleth, Paul "Doc" Evans, Ben Hagglund, David Ignatow, Calvin C. Hernton,

Ruth Lechlitner, John Rood, Robert Traver, Peter Brand, Wayne Carver, Nelson Algren, and Robert Tracy.

194
Penkower, Monty N. The Federal Writers' Project; a study in government patronage of the arts. Urbana, University of Illinois Press [1977] 266 p.

PS228.F43P4 MRR Alc

Bibliographic footnotes. Bibliography: p. [249]-258.

195
Rapport, Leonard. How valid are the Federal Writers' Project life stories: an iconoclast among the true believers. In Oral history review. 1979. [n.p.] Oral History Association. p. 33-39. D16.O68 1979

Describes his personal experiences in supervising FWP "writers" who were collecting "life stories." As the tales were written and rewritten they became increasingly fictional and removed from the original telling.

"Replies . . ." by Tom E. Terrill and Jerrold Hirsch appear in the 1980 issue.

196
Roskolenko, Harry. When I was last on Cherry Street. New York, Stein and Day [1965] 248 p. PS3535.O732Z5

"Writers' Project": p. 150-155.

Retrospective account of experiences on the New York City project.

197
Soapes, Thomas F. The Federal Writers' Project slave interviews: useful data or misleading source. In Oral history review. 1977. [n.p.] Oral History Association. p. 33-38. D16.O68 1977

Bibliographic footnotes.

198

Stott, William. Documentary expression and thirties America. New York, Oxford University Press, 1973. xvi, 361 p. illus.

F92.U5S75

The misery of the Depression was often depicted by techniques common to the period such as nonfictional literature and realistic photographs. The documentary product, while apparently objective in its information, often delivered a strong emotional impact. In their seemingly endless collecting of facts, the WPA writers reflected the documentary trend.

199

Swados, Harvey, ed. The American writer and the Great Depression. Indianapolis, Bobbs-Merrill [1966] xli, 521 p. illus.

PS536.S9

Introduction: p. xi-xxxvi. "Selected Bibliography": p. xxxviii-xli.

Selections of prose, poetry, and fiction from the period, with individual introductions. Swados notes that one effect of the Depression was to spread misery nation-wide, creating a growing sense of unity across the country. The writers' project as it probed into local history contributed to this awakening of national awareness.

200

Taber, Ronald W. Vardis Fisher and the "Idaho Guide": preserving culture for the New Deal. Pacific Northwest quarterly, v. 59, Apr. 1968: 68-76. illus., port.

F886.W28, v. 59

201

Taber, Ronald W. Writers on relief: the making of the Washington guide, 1935-1941. Pacific northwest quarterly, v. 61, Oct. 1970: 185-192. illus. F886.W28, v. 61

202

Yezierska, Anzia. Red ribbon on a white horse. New York, Charles Scribner's sons, 1950. 220 p. PS3547.E95Z53

Part Three (p. 137-197) is a colorful, retrospective, firsthand account of her days on the Federal Writers' Project in New York City.

Historical records survey workers taking inventory of old records and books

VI

Out of the Dust: The Historical Records Survey

The need to find work relief for thousands of clerical and white collar workers made jobless by the Depression coincided with a maturing interest in the archival profession and an increased awareness of the need for orderly preservation of government records (both national and local). Historians had become concerned that many records were essentially lost to researchers because their existence had not been recorded and was not known.

Robert C. Binkley, professor and historian, foresaw in imaginative detail the multiple uses to which a completed survey of records (national, state, county, and town) could be put. He attracted the interest of Luther Evans, an enthusiastic young man who was looking for a job following the receipt of his Ph.D. Evans in turn submitted proposals for the project to Harry Hopkins, urging its appropriateness for work relief. When the project was accepted, Evans became its first national director.

In 1935 the Historical Records Survey was located administratively under the Federal Writers' Project, but in November 1936 it was made an independent unit under Federal One. Its principal objective was the inventory and description of county records (or town records in New England) in each state. While critics might doubt that amateur clericals could perform valuable historical work, Evans and Binkley insisted that with adequate instruction, standardization of task demands, and close supervision the job could be done.

The first task of survey workers newly arrived at a courthouse or other repository was to locate the records and arrange them in an orderly fashion for description. It was not always easy. Many stories are told of records that were oil-drenched, worm-eaten, faded, brittle, stashed in hard-to-reach places, and even used to fire up the furnace. After the records had been arranged and described, a full report was to be written giving a brief history of the county, a summary of legal history regarding the records that were to be kept, maps, diagrams of record file locations, and other background material. Finished reports were mimeographed and distributed in limited quantities.

Additional projects were conceived and carried out with some degree of success. Among these was the American Imprints Inventory. Workers on this project went into libraries across the country to make a record of all books found in the collections that had been printed before a given date (1877 in the east and 1890 in some western states). When these book descriptions were sorted at some central point, an account of early books published in each state could be compiled, as well as a list of books' locations. This inventory of imprints was the pet project of Douglas C. McMurtrie, a scholar in the history of printing.

In lesser measure the HRS was also concerned with inventories of manuscripts and personal papers and surveys of church archives. Some local units attempted individual projects, including copying old manuscripts, recording graveyard and tombstone information, cataloging customs records (particularly in seaport towns), listing portraits painted in the locale, cumulating the messages and papers of recent Presidents, collecting book reviews for an annotated bibliography of American history, listing and indexing newspaper files, and compiling a bibliography of material by and about American authors.

Though less colorful than the art projects that were lodged with it under Federal One, the HRS earned good reviews. It was the most economical of the projects, generated little controversy, produced useful products, demonstrated how untrained workers could be employed, and developed a methodology for archival description that became a model for the profession.

"At the Time": Pre-1943 Publications

203
Blegen, Theodore C. Some aspects of historical work under the New Deal. Mississippi Valley historical review, v. 21, Sept. 1934: 195-206.   E171.J87, v. 21
    Describes early projects sponsored by the Civil Works Administration and regional historical societies that were forerunners of HRS work.

204
Blinn, Harold E. W.P.A. prepares tools for historical research in Washington state. Pacific Northwest quarterly, v. 30, Oct. 1939: 387-398.   F886.W28, v. 30
    In addition to description of HRS projects, Blinn also refers to the variety of clerical tasks of the FWP that are under way in the Northwest.

205
Bowman, Francis J. Historical Records Survey. Pacific historical review, v. 6, Mar. 1937: 67-71.   F851.P18, v. 6
    Includes names of regional officials with additional information about some of them.

206
Child, Sargent B. Status and plans for completion of the inventories of the Historical Records Survey. In Archives and libraries. 1940. Chicago, American Library Association. p. 12-25.   CD3020.A7 1940
    Also issued in Newark, by the Historical Records Survey in 1941 (12 leaves CD3020. H6C45 1941).

207
Eliot, Margaret S. Inventories and guides to historical manuscript collections. In Archives and libraries. 1940. Chicago, American Library Association. p. 26-35.
                CD3020.A7 1940

208
Eliot, Margaret S. The manuscript program of the Historical Records Survey. In American Library Association. Committee on Public Documents. Public documents with Archives and libraries. 1938. Chicago, American Library Association. p. 317-326.
                Z7164.G7A4, 1938

209
Evans, Luther H. Archival progress in the Historical Records Survey. In Society of American Archivists. Proceedings. 1936/37. Urbana, Ill. p. 90-95.
                CD1.S6, 1936/37
    With a description of the annotated bibliography of American history.

210
Evans, Luther H. Archives as materials for the teaching of history. Indiana history bulletin, v. 15, Feb. 1938: 136-153.
                F521.I367, v. 15

211
Evans, Luther H. The future program of the Historical Records Survey. In Archives and libraries. 1939. Chicago, American Library Association. p. 22-27.
                CD3020.A7, 1939

211
Evans, Luther H. The future program of the Historical Records Survey. In Archives and libraries. 1939. Chicago, American Library Association. p. 22-27.
CD3020.A7, 1939

212
Evans, Luther H. Government and local history. Pacific historical review, v. 8, Mar. 1939: 97-104.   F851.P18, v. 8
On the role of government in historical research and publication with descriptions of the Historical Records Survey and American Imprints Inventory.

213
Evans, Luther H. The Historical Records Survey. In American Library Association. Committee on Public Documents. Public documents, with Archives and libraries. 1936. Chicago, American Library Association. p. 209-212.   Z7164.G7A4, 1936

214
Evans, Luther H. The Historical Records Survey and its progress in New England. New Haven, Historical Records Survey, 1939. 18 leaves.   CD3020.H6E88

215
Evans, Luther H. The local archives program of the WPA Historical Records Survey. In American Library Association. Committee or Public Documents. Public documents, with Archives and libraries. 1938. Chicago, American Library Association. p. 284-300.   Z7164.G7A4, 1938

216
Evans, Luther H. Next steps in the improvement of local archives. In American Library Association. Committee on Public Documents. Public documents, with Archives and libraries. 1937. Chicago, American Library Association. p. 276-285.
Z7164.G7A4, 1937

217
Evans, Luther H. WPA fashions new tools for research. Washington, D.C., Historical Records Survey [1938] 16 leaves.
E175.8.E94

218
Field, Alston G. The Historical Records Survey in Illinois. In Illinois State Historical Society. Journal, v. 30, July 1937: 264-269.
F536.I18, v. 30

219
Goedecke, Karl. Accomplishments and future programs of the Pennsylvania Historical Records Survey. Pennsylvania history, v. 7, Oct. 1940: 236-242.   F146.P597, v. 7

220
Hamer, Philip M. Federal archives outside of the District of Columbia. In Society of American Archivists. Proceedings, 1936/37. Urbana, Ill. p. 83-89.
CD1.S6, 1936/37
The Federal Archives Survey was a parallel effort, administered in part by the National Archives but supported by WPA funds.

221
Historical Records Survey. Illinois. The Historical Records Survey and the political scientist. Prepared by Herbert R. Rifkind. Chicago, Ill., 1940. 16 p.   CD3020.H58

222
Historical Records Survey. Louisiana. Report on the Louisiana statewide records

project and Historical Records Survey. Foreword by Edwin A. Davis. University, La., Dept. of Archives, Louisiana State University, 1940. 22 leaves.

CD3261.H52 1940

L.C. copy imperfect: t.p. and leaf 22 wanting. Title from NUC.

Prepared by J. C. L. Andreassen.

223

Historical Records Survey. New Jersey. The Historical Records Survey in New Jersey. Description of its purpose, account of its accomplishments, bibliography of its publications. Newark, Historical Records Survey, 1941. 66 leaves.   CD3380.H6A5

"Publications of the New Jersey Historical Records Survey project": leaves [65]-66.

224

The Historical Records Survey and state archives survey of Florida. Florida historical quarterly, v. 17, July 1938: 59-63.

F306.F65, v. 17

225

Hogan, William R. The Historical Records Survey: an outside view. University, La., Dept. of Archives, Louisiana State University, 1939. 17 leaves.   CD3020.H6H6

226

Hulbert, Herman. The WPA Historical Records Survey in Oregon. Commonwealth review, v. 19, Nov. 1937: 251-260.

HC107.O7C8, v. 19

227

Kellar, Herbert A. An appraisal of the Historical Records Survey. In Archives and libraries. 1940. Chicago, American Library Association. p. 44-59.   CD3020.A7, 1940

228

Kidder, Robert W. Historical Records Survey: activities and publications. Library quarterly, v. 13, Apr. 1943: 136-149.

Z671.L713, v. 13

229

Lacy, Dan M. The Historical Records Survey and the librarian. Newark, Historical Records Survey, 1941. 19 leaves.

CD3020.H6L2

230

Larson, Cedric. The Historical Records Survey. Wilson bulletin for librarians, v. 13, Nov. 1938: 187, 192.   Z1217.W75, v. 13

231

McFarland, George M. Archives and local administrative history. American archivist, v. 4, July 1941: 170-177.

CD3020.A45, v. 4

Successful processing of archival records depends on a knowledge of the legal specifications of what records were to be kept and a familiarity with the recording practices of the clerks.

232

Morris, Richard B. [Review of HRS inventories of county archives and miscellaneous state and local archives] American historical review, v. 45, Oct. 1939: 159-162.

E171.A57, v. 45

Offers suggestions for streamlining the survey process to secure speedier publication.

233

Perry, Merrill C. The Historical Records Survey and its progress in Vermont. In Vermont Historical Society. Proceedings, new ser., v. 7, Sept. 1939: 161-177.

F46.V55, n.s., v. 7

A historical records survey worker in the Utah County Courthouse, Ogden, Utah

234

Portner, Stuart. [Michigan Historical Records Survey] Michigan history magazine, v. 24, spring 1940: 278-279.

F561.M57, v. 24

235

Rainwater, Percy L. The Historical Records Survey in Mississippi. Journal of Mississippi history, v. 1, Apr. 1939: 77-81.

F336.J68, v. 1

236

Roach, George W. Final report: the Historical Records Survey in upstate New York, 1936-1942. New York history, v. 24, Jan. 1943: 39-55. F116.N865, v. 24

237

Roach, George W. The Historical Records Survey in New York state. New York history, v. 21, Apr. 1940: 187-192.

F116.N865, v. 21

238

Scammell, J. Marius. Historical Records Survey progress report, 1938-39. In Archives and libraries. 1939. Chicago, American Library Association. p. 11-21.

CD3020.A7, 1939

239

Scammell, J. Marius. Librarians and archives. Library quarterly, v. 9, Oct. 1939: 432-444.

Z671.L713, v. 9

Public officials need education in the importance of keeping reliable archives where material can be easily retrieved. The popular view too often confuses archival material with historical manuscripts and archival functions with those of historical societies, libraries, and museums.

240

Schilling, George E. The Survey of Federal Archives in Mississippi. Journal of Mississippi history, v. 1, Oct. 1939: 207-216.

F336.J68, v. 1

241

Stephenson, Jean, and Ellen S. Woodward. Rediscovering the nation's records. Daughters of the American Revolution magazine, v. 70, Nov. 1936: 1148-1152.

E202.5.A12, v. 70

In 1935 the D.A.R. was ready to undertake a nationwide inventory of local records using their chapter members as volunteer workers.

"Looking Back": Post-1943 Publications

242

Bowie, Chester W. The Wisconsin Historical Records Survey, then and now. American archivist, v. 37, Apr. 1974: 247-261.

CD3020.A45, v. 37

243

Farran, Don. The Historical Records Survey in Iowa, 1936-1942. Annals of Iowa, 3d ser., v. 42, spring 1975: 597-608.

F616.A6, 3d s., v. 42

244

Hanson, James A. The Historical Records Survey in Wyoming, 1936-1942. Annals of Wyoming, v. 45, spring 1973: 69-91.

F756.A67, v. 45

245

Morrison, Perry D. Everyman's archive: Robert C. Binkley and the Historical Records Survey. Call number, v. 18, spring 1957: 4-9. Z733.O68, v. 18

246

Papenfuse, Edward C. 'A modicum of commitment': the present and future importance of the Historical Records Survey. American archivist, v. 37, Apr. 1974: 211-221. CD3020.A45, v. 37

247

Peterson, Trudy H. The Iowa Historical Records Survey, 1936-1942. American archivist, v. 37, Apr. 1974: 223-245.
CD3020.A45, v. 37

248

Smiley, David L. A slice of life in Depression America: the records of the Historical Records Survey. Prologue, v. 3, winter 1971: 153-159. illus. CD3020.P75, v. 3

249

Smiley, David L. The W.P.A. Historical Records Survey. In Hesseltine, William B., and Donald R. McNeil, eds. In support of Clio; essays in memory of Herbert A. Kellar. Madison, State Historical Society of Wisconsin, 1958. p. 3-28. D6.H4

AMERICAN IMPRINTS INVENTORY

250

Bruntjen, Scott. Source documents for American bibliography: three "McMurtrie manuals." Halifax, N.S., Dalhousie University, University Libraries-School of Library Service, 1978. [80] leaves.
Z1216.B78

A description of the mechanics of fieldwork for the American Imprints Inventory is followed by retyped copies of instruction manuals written for workers by Douglas C. McMurtrie and his staff.

251

McMurtrie, Douglas C. The bibliography of American imprints. Publishers' weekly, v. 144, Nov. 20, 1943: 1939-1944.
Z1219.P98, v. 144

"American Imprints Inventory Check Lists": p. 1942-1944.
- - - - - - - - - Offprint. Chicago, 1943. 8 p.
Z1250.M3

252

McMurtrie, Douglas C. Further progress in the record of American printing. In Archives and libraries. 1940. Chicago, American Library Association. p. 36-43.
CD3020.A7, 1940
- - - - - - - - - Offprint. [Chicago, 1940?] 12 p. Z1215.H67M16

253

McMurtrie, Douglas C. Locating the printed source materials for United States history. With a bibliography of lists of regional imprints. Mississippi Valley historical review, v. 31, Dec. 1944: 369-406. E171.J87, v. 31
"American Imprints Inventory Check Lists": p. 403-406.

254

McMurtrie, Douglas C. A nationwide inventory of American imprints under WPA auspices. In American Library Association. Committee on Public Documents. Public documents, with Archives and libraries. 1938. Chicago, American Library Association. p. 300-316. Z7164.G7A4, 1938
- - - - - - - - - Offprint. Chicago, Priv. print.
Z1215.H67M2

255

McMurtrie, Douglas C. A record of Washington imprints, 1853-1876. Pacific Northwest quarterly, v. 34, Jan. 1943: 27-38.
F886.W28, v. 34
Review of *A Check List of Washington Imprints, 1853-1876,* edited by Geraldine Beard.

A WPA band in San Antonio, Texas

VII

Keep America Singing: The Federal Music Project

A familiar image in discussions of work relief for artists is that of the violinist who was forced to work with pick and shovel until his sensitive fingers grew coarse and lost their music. Freeing him from the shovel and providing relevant jobs for other unemployed instrumentalists, singers, and music teachers was the role of the Federal Music Project, which was organized in 1935 under the direction of Nikolai Sokoloff.

From the beginning the project had a dual nature. Its mission directed it to serve the public and at the same time to maintain high professional standards for the performance of serious music. To bring music to the people, FMP organized free and inexpensive concerts, music lessons for poor adults, and appreciation training for children. The teaching program was concerned with training music teachers as well as pupils and practiced techniques for group instruction, such as using dummy keyboards in piano class.

The professional performer auditioned for a place in newly formed orchestras that would play a classical and modern repertoire in cities that had not known live symphonic music. Some of these orchestras, such as the Buffalo Symphony, would survive the demise of the WPA to become independent units. There were also FMP bands, dance and theater orchestras, chamber ensembles, vocal groups, Negro choruses, and opera groups. Summer performances in the park were popular, and any high school auditorium could become the site of a musical evening, sometimes presented by a traveling orchestra.

In New York the Composers' Forum Laboratory, a workshop to encourage new musical composition by American artists, was begun and the idea spread to other cities. A composer whose work was chosen for the laboratory could rehearse the performers and conduct the orchestra so that the piece was played or sung by trained musicians as the composer intended it. Following the performance the audience would discuss the work, asking questions and making suggestions. The laboratory offered valuable training and feedback for young composers and music students. In their discussions the audience and composers regularly found themselves trying to define the distinct or characteristic nature of American music; generally they found more questions than definitions.

Nonperformers also found employment with FMP as copyists and librarians, who prepared and cataloged musical scores. An index to American composers, with biographical material and composition record for each, was begun but never finished. Some workers compiled catalogs of compositions in local libraries.

One of the less controversial of the arts projects, the FMP escaped most of the congressional criticism and charges of Communist infiltration that were aimed at the artists and actors. This was due in part to the abstract and content-free nature of the musical form, and in part to the fact that WPA musicians generally did not play political music. Competitors in the Composers' Forum might favor contemporary music with intricate tonal structures and dissonance, but they did not write songs of protest or marching tunes for the radical left.

"At the Time": Pre-1943 Publications

256
Carter, Elliott. Coolidge crusade; WPA; New York season. Modern music, v. 16, Nov./Dec. 1938: 33-38.   ML1.M178, v. 16
      Elizabeth Sprague Coolidge continues to sponsor concerts featuring the music of

modern and innovative composers. The Composers' Forum-Laboratory has played a range of works for a limited audience but has made little progress toward defining an intrinsically American music.

257
Cohn, Arthur. Americans in the Fleisher collection. Modern music, v. 16, Jan./Feb. 1939: 116-119.　　　ML1.M178, v. 16
　　Brief description of a WPA music copyist program, sponsored by Edwin Fleisher of Philadelphia, to create permanent copies of unpublished orchestral work by American composers.

258
Federal music and drama projects. Musician, v. 41, Sept. 1936: 139.　　ML1.M94, v. 41
　　Strong editorial defense of government support for music and musicians, even at the risk of "socialization."

259
Federal Music Project. Current history, v. 49, Sept. 1938: 42-44. illus.　　D410.C8, v. 49
　　Brief text with six illustrations and a table showing distribution of WPA musicians by type of project on which employed.

260
Glore, Harry F. The new alphabet challenges our cities. In Music Educators National Conference. Yearbook. 1936. Chicago, p. 381-383.　　ML27.U5M67, 1936
　　Several government agencies provided music education opportunities for both teachers and students.

261
Howard, John T. Better days for music.

Harpers magazine, v. 174, Apr. 1937: 483-491.　　　AP2.H3, v. 174
　　Observes a spreading revival of interest in music which he attributes to radio broadcasting and to an increase in amateur participation in music-making, both of which have enhanced the public's desire to hear live music performed well. He regards attendance at WPA concerts as evidence for, but not a cause of, the revival; he does not mention the work of the WPA in music education for adults.

262
Hughes, Edwin, comp. Forum: the effect of WPA projects on the work of the private piano teacher. In Music Teachers National Association. Volume of proceedings. 1936. Oberlin, Ohio, 1937. p. 144-153.
　　　ML27.U5M8, 1936
　　Expressions of fear and concern voiced by participants at the annual meeting, along with a defense of the design and intent of the Federal Music Project.

263
McFarland, Frances. Federal Music Project in New York City. In Music Educators National Conference. Yearbook. 1936. Chicago. p. 384-388.　　ML27.U5M67, 1936

264
Maier, Guy. Federal Music Project's contribution to American music. In Music Educators National Conference. Yearbook. 1938. Chicago. p. 96-99.　　ML27.U5M67, 1938

265
Moore, Earl V. Choral music and the WPA music program. In Music Teachers National Association. Volume of proceedings. 1939. Pittsburgh, 1940. p. 334-338.
　　　ML27.U5M8, 1939

San Antonio, Texas, band

266
Moore, Earl V. Men, music, and morale: the case for the federal project. Musical America, v. 62, Apr. 25, 1942: 5, 41. illus.
ML1.M384, v. 62

267
Moore, Earl V. The WPA music program—plans and activities. In Music Teachers National Association. Volume of proceedings. 1939. Pittsburgh, 1940. p. 373-384.
ML27.U5M8, 1939

268
Overmeyer, Grace. The musician starves. American mercury, v. 32, June 1934: 224-231.
AP2.A37, v. 32

269
Pettis, Ashley. The WPA and the American composer. Musical quarterly, v. 26, Jan. 1940: 101-112.
ML1.M725, v. 26
Through its program of performing and analyzing native American works, the Composers' Forum-Laboratory has shown notable achievement in the "encouragement of musical compositions and in the definition of a living American music."

270
Pride of New York City WPA: a 95-man symphony orchestra. Newsweek, v. 17, Mar. 31, 1941: 63. illus.
AP2.N6772, v. 17

271
Sokoloff, Nikolai. America's vast new musical awakening. Etude, v. 55, Apr. 1937: 221-222. port.
ML1.E8, v. 55

272
Sokoloff, Nikolai. The Federal Music Project. In Music Teachers National Association.

Volume of proceedings. 1936. Oberlin, Ohio, 1937. p. 56-62.
ML27.U5M8, 1936

273
Sokoloff, Nikolai. What the Federal Music Project is doing in education. In Music Educators National Conference. Yearbook. 1936. Chicago. p. 379-381.
ML27.U5M67, 1936

274
WPA melody for twenty millions: Federal Music Project. Literary digest, v. 122, Sept. 19, 1936: 22.
AP2.L58, v. 122

"Looking Back": Post-1943 Publications

275
Canon, Cornelius B. Art for whose sake: the Federal Music Project of the WPA, by Neal Canon. In Challenges in American culture. Edited by Ray B. Browne, Larry N. Landrum [and] William K. Bottorff. Bowling Green, Ohio. Bowling Green University Press [1970] p. [85]-100
E169.1.C43

276
Canon, Cornelius B. The Federal Music Project of the Works Progress Administration: music in a democracy. 1963. 304 (i.e., 307) p.
Micro AC-1, no. 63-7915
Thesis (Ph. D.)—University of Minnesota.
Abstracted in *Dissertation Abstracts*, v. 24, Nov. 1963, p. 2068-2069.

277
Denisoff, R. Serge. Great day coming; folk music and the American left. Urbana, University of Illinois Press [1971] 219 p. ports.
ML3795.D34

Includes information on the songs of protest marchers, labor organizers, and other dissidents of the thirties.

278

Mehren, Peter. San Diego's opera unit of the WPA Federal Music Project. Journal of San Diego history, v. 18, summer 1972: 12-21.　　　　　　F868.S15J6, v. 18

279

Solomon, Izler. A decade to defeat decadence. Musical courier, v. 151, Feb. 1, 1955: 46-48. illus.　　　　ML1.M43, v. 151

An overview of the Music Project's activities particularly with regard to composers.

280

Spaeth, Sigmund G. A history of popular music in America. New York, Random House [1948] xv, 729 p.　　　ML2811.S7

"The Tired Thirties": p. 477-524.

Does not deal specifically with the Federal Music Project, but does give some background information about the period and its memorable composers and performers.

281

Warren-Findley, Janelle J. Of tears and need: the Federal Music Project, 1935-1943. 1973.

Thesis (Ph.D.)—George Washington University.

282

Woodworth, William H. The Federal Music Project of the Works Progress Administration in New Jersey. 1970. 206 p.

Micro AC-1, no. 71-4550

Thesis (Ed. D.)—University of Michigan.

Abstracted in *Dissertation Abstracts International*, v. 31A, Feb. 1971, p. 4211.

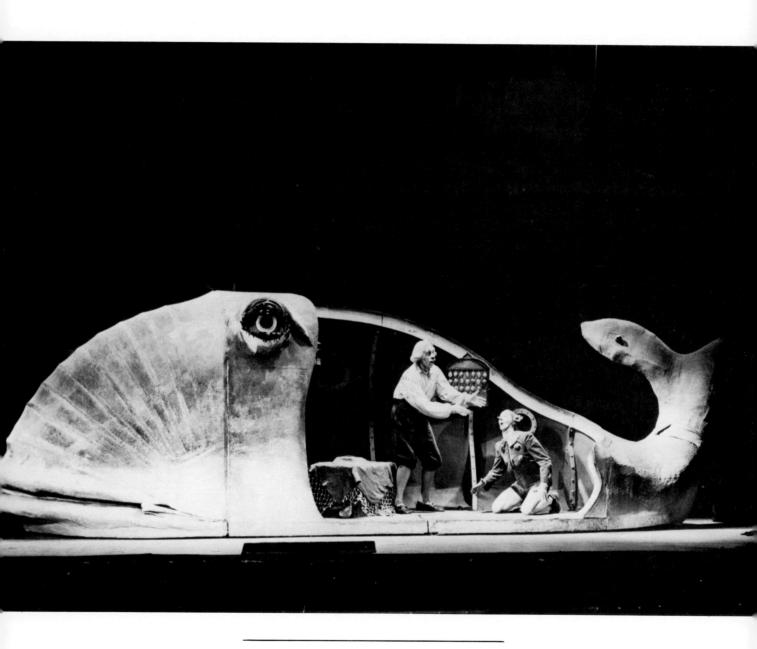

Pinocchio on stage, a New York City production

VIII

Work Relief on Stage: The Federal Theatre Project

The Federal Theatre Project was, in many respects, the most visible and the most controversial of the Federal One projects. In its array of works it provided something for everyone: circus, vaudeville, classical and contemporary drama, ethnic theater, musical comedy, marionette shows, CCC camp performances, experimental stage works, social protest drama, modern dance, and traveling troupes of players. Its critics charged that federal theater was radical, immoral, wasteful, nonproductive, and Communist-dominated. Its advocates claimed that the project created aesthetically exciting productions, saved the skills of thousands of performers and technicians, and brought to widespread audiences the thrill of living theater that many had never experienced before.

To direct the project Harry Hopkins chose Hallie Flanagan, the guiding hand behind the Experimental Theatre at Vassar. That energetic and enthusiastic young woman (who was married to Philip H. Davis, a supportive and understanding husband, but retained the name of her first husband in her professional role) immersed herself in the demanding task of organizing WPA theater. Taking encouragement from Elmer Rice and other innovators, she drew up a plan for dividing the country into regional units, each with its own director, each drawing stimulation from its own locale, and each making jobs for local theater personnel who were on relief. While they floundered with the paperwork and red tape that were always a part of work relief programs, Mrs. Flanagan and her associates dreamed of building a truly national theater that would produce artistically and socially important drama of professional quality and regional identity.

Despite the emphasis on nationwide activity, the New York City project blossomed first, probably because so much of American theatrical activity was already centered there. In its first year it presented the premier performance of T. S. Eliot's *Murder in the Cathedral.* Another unit worked on developing documentary plays on timely topics such as farm problems or the faults of public utilities, that were called Living Newspapers. With action and dialogue drawn from the daily news, their scripts did not hesitate to step on the toes of businessmen and politicians. The productions were well suited to work relief, for they needed a minimum of sets, relying on lighting and staging for their effectiveness. Further, they used a large number of players, and they dealt with problems such as poverty and housing that were familiar to actors on relief.

In Harlem the Negro unit under the guidance of John Houseman and Rose McClendon led off with *Walk Together Chillun* while planning a Shakespearian tragedy. The latter evolved into a *Macbeth* whose locale had been shifted to Haiti and whose witches had been transformed into voodoo-chanting spellsters. Directed by Orson Welles, it was a dynamic and colorful production that was sold out for months and later was sent to tour in other cities.

Progress in the rest of the country seemed slower. However, in a determined demonstration of the potential scope of federal theater, joint productions of Sinclair Lewis' *It Can't Happen Here* were undertaken. On October 27, 1936, the play opened simultaneously in twenty-one theaters in seventeen states. There were three productions in New York City: one in Yiddish, one by the Suitcase Theatre on Staten Island, and the "standard" version at the Adelphi Theatre.

Despite its apparent success, the Federal Theatre Project was doomed, almost from

51

the beginning, to an early death. Its enemies were powerful and determined. In the House of Representatives the Committee on Un-American Activities, chaired by Martin Dies of Texas, sought to sniff out Communists and claimed to find them in the federal arts projects. Although the directors testified in defense of their programs, their explanations were diluted by the committee's interrogatory tactics.

When Congress began deliberations on WPA appropriations for 1939-40, the sessions of criticism aimed at the FTP became particularly vitriolic. It was said that the productions were "putrid" and designed only to spread Kremlin propaganda at the expense of American taxpayers. Congressmen rose to ridicule even the titles of plays, finding them silly and immoral.

Newspaper theater critics responded with a joint message rebutting the charges of poor quality, while movie stars and famous stage personalities praised the work of the federal theater and called for its extension. Although the project had more supporters in the Senate than in the House, critics could not be outweighed. Overall, allocations for the WPA were cut. The other projects of Federal One were reduced to local programs dependent on finding sponsors and support. The Federal Theatre Project was terminated outright, receiving just a brief extension for finishing up.

The lights went out on federal theater on June 30, 1939. At the Ritz Theatre in New York the cast of *Pinocchio* altered its ending to symbolize the project's fate. As the actors chanted his dirge, the wooden puppet failed to spring to life as a real boy. Pinocchio was dead.

"At the Time": Pre-1943 Publications

283

Calverton, Victor F. The cultural barometer [the Federal Theatre Project] Current history, v. 46, June 1937: 88-93. illus.

D410.C8, v. 46

Describes and defends the project, asserting that it "has put on plays which no Broadway producer had the 'guts' or insight to produce."

284

Davis, Hallie Flanagan. Arena. New York, Duell, Sloane and Pearce [1940] 475 p. illus.   PN2266.D37

"Production Record and Financial Statement": p. [375]-436. Bibliography: p. 439-447.

Narrative account of her impressions and experiences while she was director of the Federal Theatre Project.

285

Davis, Hallie Flanagan. Theatre and geography. American magazine of art, v. 31, Aug. 1938: 464-468. illus.   N1.M25, v. 31

Discusses implications of expanding federal theater across the nation. While centralized planning is essential, one region should not be allowed to dominate the others. "Only through dramatic development of each state and region in a nationwide pattern is it possible to develop a theatre reflecting and enriching our country."

286

Davis, Hallie Flanagan. A theatre for the people. American magazine of art, v. 29, Aug. 1946: 494-503. illus.   N1.M25, v. 29

Though commenting primarily on the theater, the author notes cooperation among the several projects of Federal One. WPA musicians and writers contribute to performances, while government-sponsored art hangs in the lobbies.

287
Fiske, Harrison G. The federal theater doomboggle. Saturday evening post, v. 209, Aug. 1, 1936: 23, 68-72. illus.

AP2.S2, v. 209

In its first eight months of operation the FTP has spent hundreds of thousands of dollars on a "dozen paltry productions." Mrs. Flanagan wants to "Russianize" the drama and the project's "hair is full of Communists."

288
Garrett, Garet. Federal theater for the masses. Saturday evening post, v. 208, June 20, 1936: 8-9, 84-86, 88. illus.

AP2.S2, v. 208

In the Living Newspaper production of *Triple A Plowed Under* are woven strands of Communist doctrine that might be overlooked by the politically naive. The terms "hunger" and "starvation," which are heavily underscored in the play, are "logotypes of Communist propaganda." The ending, which prophesies cooperation between farmers and consumers, is identical to the announced Communist goal of developing a national workers and farmers labor party.

289
Gassner, John. Theatre for the people. Current history, v. 1, Oct. 1941: 185-188.

D410.C82, v. 1

In his defense of FTP's accomplishments Gassner asserts that "If your theatre is now poorer for having lost this adjunct to the professional field, it would be still poorer today if the project had never existed."

290
Gilder, Rosamond. The federal theatre, a record. Theatre arts monthly, v. 20, June 1936: 430-438.   PN1560.T392, v. 20

Project directors have learned their way around bureaucratic obstacles and are moving ahead with enthusiasm.

291
Kolodin, Irving. Footlights, federal style: the astonishing story of the federal theater. Harpers magazine, v. 173, Nov. 1936: 621-631.   AP2.H3, v. 173

292
Lavery, Emmet. Communism and the federal theatre. Commonweal, v. 28, Oct. 7, 1938: 610-612.   AP2.C6897, v. 28

Refutes charges of Communist infiltration into the WPA theater project by pointing out that a majority of the plays produced were conventional and classical rather than radical. Even those that dramatized social problems did not propose Marxist solutions.

293
Noble, Vernon. Art out of hunger. National review, v. 112, Apr. 1939: 482-488.

AP4.A25, v. 112

294
Powell, Anne. Federal children's theater in New York City. Recreation, v. 30, Oct. 1936: 344-345, 372-373. illus.

GV421.R5, v. 30

295
Whitman, Willson. Bread and circuses; a study of the federal theatre. New York,

Oxford University Press, 1937, 191 p.
                                    PN2266.W44
Bibliography: p. [173]-174. "Representative Productions of Federal Theatre, from a National Survey Not Yet Completed": p. [175]-191.

296

Wittler, Clarence J. Some social trends in WPA drama. Washington, D.C., Catholic University of America Press, 1939. 125 p.
                                    PS351.W5
Thesis (Ph.D.)—Catholic University of America.
Analyzed 88 FTP plays for their comments on forms of government, economic doctrines, religion, and assorted social problems.

"Looking Back": Post-1943 Publications

297

Abramson, Doris E. Negro playwrights in the American theatre, 1925-1959. New York, Columbia University Press, 1969. 335 p.   PS351.A2
"The Thirties; the Job We Never Had": p. [44]-88.
Analysis of some of the plays and playwrights of the Negro unit of the New York FTP including their first production, *Walk Together Chillun,* by Frank Wilson and Rudolph Fisher's *Conjur Man Dies* from the 1935-36 season.

298

Brown, Lorraine. Federal theatre; melodrama, social protest, and genius. In U.S. Library of Congress. Quarterly journal, v. 36, winter 1979: 18-37. illus.
                                    Z881.U49A3, v. 36

299

Craig, Evelyn Q. Black drama of the federal theatre era: beyond the formal horizons. Amherst, University of Massachusetts Press, 1980. 239 p.   PS338.N4C7
Bibliography: p. 222-230.

300

France, Richard. The 'Voodoo' *Macbeth* of Orson Welles. Yale/theatre, [v. 5, no. 3] 1974: 66-78.   PN2000.Y34 [v. 5]

301

Heymann, Jeanne L. Dance in the Depression: the WPA project. Dance scope, v. 9, spring/summer 1975: 28-40. illus.
                                    GV1580.D32, v. 9

302

Goldstein, Malcolm. The political stage: American drama and theater of the Great Depression. New York, Oxford University Press, 1974. 482 p. illus.
                                    PS338.P6G6
"The Federal Theater, 1935-1939": p. [241]-292.

303

Himelstein, Morgan Y. Drama was a weapon: the left-wing theatre in New York, 1929-1941. With a foreword by John Gassner. New Brunswick, N.J., Rutgers University Press [1963] 300 p. illus.   PN2277.N545
"Federal Theatre": p. 85-112.
Discusses the social drama of the FTP and estimates the extent of Communist influence within the project.

304

Holcomb, Robert. The federal theatre in Los Angeles. California historical quarterly, v. 41, June 1962: 131-147. F856.C24, v. 41

305

Houseman, John. Run-through; a memoir. New York, [1972] 507 p. illus.

PN2287.H7A3

"WPA Negro Theatre": p. 173-210.

As director of the Harlem-based project, the author describes the rehearsal and production of the "Voodoo *Macbeth*."

306

McDermott, Douglas. The living newspaper as a dramatic form. Modern drama, v. 8, May 1965: 82-94.   PN1861.M55, v. 8

307

Mathews, Jane D. The federal theatre, 1935-1939: plays, relief, and politics. Princeton, N.J., Princeton University Press, 1967. 342 p. illus.   PN2266.M33

Bibliography: p. 315-331.

Considers the paradox of federal theater—that it was on the one hand a work relief plan for the impoverished and on the other an innovation in government support for a national art program. Mathews analyzes the project as a national institution, describing "its origins and administration, the personalities, ideas, and circumstances which shaped it, the problems it faced, and the contributions it made."

308

Maurer, Joyce C. Federal theatre in Cincinnati. In Cincinnati Historical Society. Bulletin, v. 32, spring/summer 1974: 28-45. illus.   F486.H653, v. 32

Includes bibliographic references.

309

Rabkin, Gerald. Drama and commitment; politics in the American theatre of the thirties. Bloomington, Indiana University Press, 1964.   PS338.P6R3

"A Selected Bibliography": p. 297-300. Bibliographic references included in "Notes" (p. 301-314).

"The Federal Theatre: Theatre Is Men Working": p. [94]-123.

Includes content analysis of many of the individual plays produced by the FTP.

310

Rice, Elmer L. The living theatre. New York, Harper [1959] 306 p.   PN2037.R5

"The Federal Theatre Project": p. 148-160.

311

Ross, Ronald. The role of blacks in the federal theatre, 1935-1939. Journal of Negro history, v. 59, Jan. 1974: 38-50.

E185.J86, v. 59

312

Smiley, Sam. Rhetoric on stage in living newspapers. Quarterly journal of speech, v. 54, Feb. 1968: 29-36. PN4071.Q3, v. 54

313

Walsh, Elizabeth E. New Deal theatre. Dramatics, v. 48, Mar./Apr. 1977: 14-19. illus.

PN3175.A1H5, v. 48

Federal theater is remembered for its innovations and for the fact that it "gave many young people a chance to experiment and kept many now-famous young professionals in the craft who might have been lost to the theatre forever."

314

Williams, Jay. Stage left. New York, Scribner's [1974] 278 p. illus.   PN2266.W5

Discusses the Federal Theatre Project in the larger framework of thirties drama, the years of agitprop, social consciousness, and revolutionary theater.

A national book fair in New York City

IX

Where Is It Now? Collectors and Collections

Most activities of the WPA arts projects were abruptly terminated by the onset of World War II. Many projects, particularly the writing tasks of the FWP and HRS, were hurriedly pushed to a temporary conclusion or were left unfinished. Forty years later the perplexing question of what became of all the WPA products is frequently raised.

No complete answer is possible, and it is difficult to estimate how much material is not accounted for. In the confusion that accompanied the conversion to wartime, local project directors disposed of their files in various ways. Some sent their records or parts of their files to the National Archives, but many other records were discarded or retained in local court houses and city buildings. Some unfinished writing was sent to local libraries, museums, or historical societies. Much uncompleted work from the Historical Records Survey was left in local depositories in the hope that it could be finished after the war. A number of artworks were thrown away or destroyed; a few paintings turned up in secondhand stores; murals were sometimes painted over or lost in building remodeling. Some works of painting and sculpture, however, still remain in public buildings.

The references that follow include lists that are descriptive of the nature and extent of WPA publications and products, articles that give some information about the treatment and disposition of WPA products, bibliographies of published material from Federal One projects, and guides to archival collections that contain WPA material. Also included are references to items (particularly from the FWP and HRS) that were collected and published after the demise of the project. Unfortunately many repositories of such material as recordings, photographs, drawings, graphics, musical scores, files of folklore, posters, unpublished writing, and archival records will not be represented here, for no published account of them was located.

NEW DEAL AND WPA

Following are references to items about the period of the New Deal and the overall operation and publication output of the WPA. The Inventory and Final Report give a broad picture of the many projects that were attempted. The bibliographies of research reports and New Deal publications are useful for determining what was written and when. It is usually difficult to locate these reports, however, for many were only mimeographed and received limited distribution.

At the Library of Congress material published by the WPA is filed under the heading "U.S. Work Projects Administration" even if the publication was prepared at an earlier date by the Works Progress Administration. Entries are further subdivided by state. Material issued by a specific unit was often cataloged under that name, such as "Federal Writers' Project" or "Writers' Program. Massachusetts."

315
Cole, John Y. WPA research materials at the Library of Congress; a review and progress report. In U.S. Library of Congress. Information bulletin, v. 33, Nov. 29, 1974: 243-245.   Z733.U57I6, v. 33

316
Failing, Patricia. Timberline lodge. Americana, v. 8, Mar./Apr. 1980: 32-38. col. illus.
          E171.A444a, v. 8

Though nearly lost to the ravages of time and weather, the resort has been restored and reopened.

317
Flynn, George Q. The New Deal and local archives: the Pacific Northwest. American archivist, v. 33, Jan. 1970: 41-52.

CD3020.A45, v. 33

A broad survey of available primary material for the study of the period in general and the WPA in particular.

318
Hickok, Lorena A. One-third of a nation: Lorena Hickok reports on the Great Depression. Edited by Richard Lowitt and Maurine Beasley. Urbana, University of Illinois Press, c1981.   DLC

As chief field investigator for Harry Hopkins, Hickok toured the country sending back weekly reports of the poverty conditions and relief efforts she observed. These reports are now collected and published together.

319
Kentucky. Division of Archives and Records Management. Inventory of the records of the Work Projects Administration in Kentucky. Compiled by Dennis L. Fielding. Frankfort, Ky., Division of Archives and Records Management, Dept. of Library and Archives, 1979. 79 leaves.

CD3256.W67K46 1979

Bibliography: leaves 75-76.

320
Peck, David. Salvaging the art and literature of the 1930's: a bibliographical essay. Centennial review, v. 20, spring 1976: 128-141.   AS30.C45, v. 20

321
U.S. Federal Emergency Relief Administration. Subject index of research bulletins and monographs issued by Federal Emergency Relief Administration and Works Progress Administration, Division of Social Research. [Washington, 1937] 110 (i.e. 121) numbered leaves, maps.

Z7164.U56U52 1937

Reprinted in Westport, Conn., by Greenwood Press in 1976 (Z7164. U56U532 1976).

322
U.S. Federal Works Agency. Final report on the WPA program, 1935-43. Washington, U.S. Govt. Print. Off. [1947] 145 p. illus.

HD3881.A565 1943g

Reprinted in Westport, Conn., by Greenwood Press in 1976 (HD3881.F43 1976).

"Publications of the WPA": p. 143-145.

323
U.S. Library of Congress. Special collections in the Library of Congress: a selective guide. Compiled by Annette Melville. Washington, The Library, 1980. xv, 464 p. illus.   Z733.U58U54

"Ex-slave Narrative Collection": p. 101-102; "Farm Security Administration [photograph] Collection": p. 107-109; "Federal Theatre Project Collection": p. 112-113; "Work Projects Administration Folklore Collection": p. 382-383; "Work Projects Administration Poster Collection": p. 384.

324
U.S. Work Projects Administration. Index of research projects. [Washington, U.S. Govt. Print. Off., 1938-39] 3 v.

HD3881.A56 1938

"Scope of materials included in this index: . . . Vol. I, Entries 1-2635. Summaries of reports on CWA, ERA, and WPA research projects received in Washington between October 1933 and December 1937 except reports resulting from projects operated under the sponsorship of public planning agencies; brief descriptions of research projects completed or in progress up to December 1937 for which no formal reports were available. Vol. II, Entries 2636-3802. Summaries of reports on research undertaken by public planning agencies from January 1933 to December 1938; includes references to all such materials (in so far as copies were available in Washington) prepared by those agencies with or without the assistance of relief personnel . . . Vol. III, Entries 3803-5137. Summaries of reports on CWA, ERA, and WPA research projects received in Washington between January 1938 and April 1939."

Reprinted in Westport, Conn., by Greenwood Press in 1976 (H83.U56 1976).

325

U.S. Work Projects Administration. Inventory. An appraisal of the results of the Works Progress Administration. [Washington, U.S. Govt. Print. Off., 1938] 100 p. illus.   TA23.A465 1938

A summary in words and pictures of the many projects on which WPA workers have been employed.

326

U.S. Work Projects Administration. W.P.A. technical series: research and records bibliography. nos. 1-8. Washington, 1940-43. 8 v.   Z1223.W85 MRR Alc

Issued by the Work Projects Adminis-

tration (nos. 1-4 by the Division of Professional and Service Projects; no. 5 by the Division of Community Service Programs; nos. 6-8 by the Division of Service Projects).

"The series of 'Bibliographies of research projects reports' supplements volumes 1, 2, and 3 of the 'Index of research projects.'"

Contents: nos. 1-3, 5-6, 8. Bibliography of research projects reports.—nos. 4, 7. Check list of Historical Records Survey publications.

327

Wilcox, Jerome K. Guide to the official publications of the New Deal administrations (mimeographed and printed). Chicago, American Library Association, 1934. 113 p.   Z1223.Z7W62

A checklist of publications from March, 1933 to April 15, 1934.

- - - - - - - - - [First] supplement. (April 15, 1934-December 1, 1935). Chicago, American Library Association, 1936. 184 p.
                    Z1223.Z7W62 Suppl.

- - - - - - - - - Second supplement. (December 1, 1935-January 1, 1937). Chicago, American Library Association, 1937. 190 p.   Z1223.Z7W62 Suppl.

328

Wilcox, Jerome K. Unemployment relief documents; guide to the official publications and releases of F.E.R.A. and the 48 state relief agencies. New York, H.W. Wilson Co., 1936. 95 p.   Z1223.Z7W64

Contents: Checklist of final state CWA reports.—Checklist of the publications and releases of the Federal Emergency Relief Administration and the Federal Surplus Relief Corporation.—Checklist of the publications and releases of the National

Youth Administration and the Works Progress Administration.—List of the publications and releases of the 48 state relief agencies (and of the territories).—Partial list of transient camp newspapers.

FEDERAL ART PROJECT

The 1970's saw a revival of interest in New Deal art. Researchers sifted the records and located many paintings. Several theses were written from such research. At the same time a number of exhibitions were prepared at art galleries and museums across the country. The Government Services Administration launched its own Fine Arts Inventory of thirties art in public buildings and turned up many paintings that had been thought lost. A group of them was given to the custody of the Smithsonian's National Collection of Fine Arts.

Guides to Archives

329
Archives of American Art. A checklist of the collection. 2d ed. rev. Washington, Archives of American Art, Smithsonian Institution, 1977. ca. 150 p.

Z6616.A2A68 1977

An edition of 1975 which was published under the title *A Checklist of the Collection, Spring 1975,* was compiled by Arthur J. Breton, Nancy H. Zembala, and Anne P. Nicastro.

A bureau of the Smithsonian Institution, the Archives collects and microfilms personal papers and records of artists, art galleries, art organizations, critics, and collectors. Material relevant to the New Deal is scattered throughout its collections.

330
McCoy, Garnett. Archives of American Art; a directory of resources. New York, Bowker, 1972. 163 p.   Z6611.A7M3

Descriptive notes on the contents of 555 record groups.

331
O'Connor, Francis V. Guide to New Deal art project documentation. In his Federal support for the visual arts: the New Deal and now. Greenwich, Conn., New York Graphic Society, 1969. p. [127]-173.

N6512.O25

"This guide is designed to facilitate searching the holdings of the National Archives related to the New Deal art projects," specifically Record Group 69 for files of the WPA and Record Group 121 for Public Building Service material.

The Search for Lost Art

332
Berman, Greta. Does 'Flight' have a future? Art in America, v. 64, Sept./Oct. 1976: 97-99. illus.   N1.A43, v. 64

A WPA/FAP mural by James Brooks at New York's La Guardia airport was painted over with 14 layers of paint, but restoration appears to be practicable.

333
Osnos, Nina F. New deal for New Deal art: national fine arts inventory. Art in America, v. 60, Jan./Feb. 1972: 19   N1.A43, v. 60

334
Yasko, Karel. Treasures from the Depression. Historic preservation, v. 24, July/Sept. 1972: 26-31. illus. (part col.)

E151.H5, v. 24

335
WPA art: rescue of a U.S. treasure. U.S. news & world report, v. 70, June 21, 1971: 75-78. illus.   JK1.V65, v. 70

Exhibitions

336
Bermingham, Peter. The New Deal in the Southwest, Arizona and New Mexico. [Tucson, University of Arizona Museum of Art. 1980?] 67 p. illus. (part col.)
                    N8838.B47
An exhibition organized by the University of Arizona Museum of Art, held at the museum, Jan. 18-Feb. 15, at Northern Arizona University Art Gallery, Mar. 27-April 28, and at Phoenix Art Museum, May 24-July 13, 1980.

337
Calcagno, Nicholas A. New Deal murals in Oklahoma; a bicentennial project. Miami, Okla., Pioneer Print. [1976] 52 p. illus. (part col.)   ND2634.O5C34Ni
Bibliography: p. 52.
A brochure designed to accompany a slide-sound program entitled "Government, New Deal Art, and the People of Oklahoma; Public Issues and Citizen Values." Included are notes on the artists and the locations of the murals mentioned.

338
DeCordova and Dana Museum and Park, Lincoln, Mass. By the people, for the people: New England. [Exhibition] September 25-November 27, 1977. Lincoln, Mass., The Museum [1977] 92 p. illus.
                    N8838.D38 1977
Contents: The art projects in New England: some recollections, by Charles H.

Sawyer.—By the people, for the people, by Edith A. Tonelli.—Catalogue: easel work, prints, murals and commissioned works, the Index of American Design, crafts and community programs.—Sources.

339
De Saisset Art Gallery and Museum. New Deal art: California. Santa Clara, Calif., De Saisset Art Gallery and Museum, University of Santa Clara [1976] 172 p. illus.
                    N8838.D4 1976
An Exhibition, Jan. 17-June 15, 1976.
Partial contents: Introduction, by Francis V. O'Connor.—Notes on the exhibition, by Charles Shere.—Farm Security Administration photographers in California, notes by Paul Hoffman.—Works Progress Administration/Federal Art Project photographers, notes by Paul Hoffman.—The New Deal and public art in California, by Steven M. Gelber.
Illustrations include selected reproductions from the exhibition.

340
Kingsbury, Martha. Art of the thirties; the Pacific Northwest. Seattle, Published for the Henry Art Gallery by the University of Washington Press [1972] 95 p. illus. (Index of art in the Pacific Northwest, no. 4)   N6528.K5
Catalog for an exhibition held at the Henry Art Gallery, University of Washington, April 1972.

341
Marling, Karal A. Federal art in Cleveland, 1933-1943, an exhibition, September 16 to November 1, 1974. [Cleveland, Cleveland Public Library, 1974] 125 p. illus.
                    N8838.M37

Bibliographic references included in "Notes" (p. 62-66).

"The Prelude: from Boom to Bust [New Deal Art in Cleveland]": p. 1-61.

342
New Muse Community Museum of Brooklyn. The Black artists in the WPA, 1933-1943. [An exhibition of drawings, paintings, and sculpture, February 15-March 30, 1976. Charlene Claye Van Derzee, curator, George Carter, assistant curator. Brooklyn, N.Y. New Muse Community Museum of Brooklyn, 1976 23 p.] illus.
N6538.N5N37 1976

343
Smithsonian Institution. Traveling Exhibition Service. WPA/FAP graphics. Washington, Published for the Smithsonian Institution Traveling Exhibition Service by the Smithsonian Institution Press, 1976. 23 p. illus. (Smithsonian Institution Press publication, no. 6217)   NE508.S58 1976

344
Taylor, Joshua C. A poignant, relevant backward look at artists of the Great Depression. Smithsonian, v. 10, Oct. 1979: 44-53. illus. (part col.)   AS30.S6, v. 10

Selections from recent exhibitions at the National Collection of Fine Arts and National Portrait Gallery with some discussion of attempts to salvage lost "WPA art."

Index of American Design

Plates from the Index were originally kept in the Metropolitan Museum of Art in New York City. However, since most of the work had been done under federal sponsorship, it was decided that Washington, D.C., was the appropriate repository. In 1944 the collection was transferred to the National Gallery. At present it is not on exhibit but is available for study by appointment.

Chadwyck Healy/Somerset House issued a ten-part color microfiche edition of 15,000 plates from the Index. This is accompanied by a printed catalog available in ten parts or in a single consolidated copy.

345
Christensen, Erwin O. The Index of American Design. Introduction by Holger Cahill. New York, Macmillan, 1950. xviii, 229 p. 378 illus. (part col.)
NK1403.C5 MRR Alc
Bibliography: p. 219-221.

An organized arrangement and description of the material in the National Gallery of Art that Cahill calls the "fullest presentation of that index so far."

346
Hornung, Clarence P. Treasury of American design; a pictorial survey of popular folk arts based upon watercolor renderings in the Index of American Design at the National Gallery of Art. Foreword by J. Carter Brown. Introduction by Holger Cahill. New York, H. N. Abrams [1972] 2 v. (xxvii, 846 p.) illus. (part col.)
NK805.H67

FEDERAL WRITERS' PROJECT

Much of the writing generated by the FWP was published, some as hardback books and some as small pamphlets that were distributed free or sold for a few cents. Most of the books of the American Guide series are available in public libraries and reprints of many state and city guides are currently offered for sale. References to bibliographies of FWP publications are included here.

Some of the first-person narratives were published while the project was still active. *These Are Our Lives* (Chapel Hill, University of North Carolina Press, 1939. 431 p.) reproduced interviews from the South. Recently additional collections of first-person narratives have been published. Many unpublished interviews apparently still reside in depositories around the country. Interviews with former slaves have been collected and published in several forms which are described in a subsection that follows. All these first-person documents can provide valuable source material for scholars if appropriate precautions are taken. Those who intend to use published narratives as primary material will want to inform themselves about the amount and type of editing the material received before publication.

Writers' Project Material
Listed and Archived

347
Colby, Merle E. Final report on disposition of unpublished materials of WPA Writers' Program, April 8, 1943. [Washington? 1943] 12 leaves.   E175.4.W9C6
Photostat reproduction (positive) made from typewritten copy.
Additional disposition of much of this material has taken place since 1943.

348
Cordova, Gilberto Benito. Bibliography of unpublished materials pertaining to Hispanic culture [in the New Mexico WPA writers' files]. Santa Fe, N.M., Bilingual-Bicultural Communicative Arts Unit, Division of Instructional Services, State Dept. of Education, 1972. 44 p.   Z5984.U6C67
Entries are arranged by author and indexed by subject.

349
Hendrickson, Gordon O. The WPA writers' project in Wyoming: history and collections. Annals of Wyoming, v. 49, fall 1977: 175-192. ports.   F756.A67, v. 49
Includes bibliographic references.

In 1976 a detailed inventory of WPA material in the Historical Research and Publications Division of the Wyoming State Archives and Historical Department was completed. Some 65 boxes of manuscripts, photographs, and administrative papers (including both FWP and HRS material) have been reviewed, organized, inventoried, and classified for researcher use. Hendrickson is the compiler of *Wyoming Works Projects Administration Federal Writers Project Collection Inventory* (Cheyenne, Wyoming, Wyoming State Archives and Historical Department, 1977).

350
Scharf, Arthur. Selected publications of the WPA Federal Writers' Project and the Writers' Program. In Mangione, Jerre G. The dream and the deal; the Federal Writers' Project 1935-1943. Boston, Little, Brown [1972] p. 375-396.
                    E175.4.W9M3
In his introduction Scharf defines his criteria for including publications. For the most part he cited only works that were actually published under the auspices of the WPA/FWP.

351
U.S. National Archives. Preliminary inventory of the records of the Federal Writers' Project, Work Projects Administration, 1935-44 (Record group 69) Compiled by Katherine H. Davidson. Washington, 1953. 15 p. (National Archives publication no. 54-2. Preliminary inventories, no. 57)
CD3026.A32 no. 57

352
Virginia. University. Library. Manuscripts Dept. An annotated listing of folklore collected by workers of the Virginia Writers' Project, Work Projects Administration, held in the Manuscripts Department at Alderman Library of the University of Virginia. Compiled by Charles L. Perdue, Jr., Thomas E. Barden, [and] Robert K. Phillips. Norwood, Pa., Norwood Editions, 1979.   DLC

353
W.P.A. folklore collection. California folklore quarterly, v. 3, July 1944: 204-244.
GR1.C26, v. 3
    Brief mention of "some twenty-three hundred files of collectanea which came to the University of California at Los Angeles upon the disbanding of the Southern California Writers' Project . . . at the end of 1942." An interview with a longtime San Francisco resident (taken as a first person narrative) is included.

354
Writers' program. Catalogue, WPA Writers' Program publications. September, 1941. [Washington, U.S. Govt. Print. Off., 1942] 54 p.   Z1236.W75 MRR Alc

Published Collections of First-Person Narratives

355
Banks, Ann. Making it through hard times. Atlantic, v. 246, July 1980: 40-44, 49-57. illus.   AP2.A8, v. 246
    Selections from first-person narratives collected by the FWP and now held at the Library of Congress.

356
Brown, Lorin W., Charles L. Briggs, and Marta Weigle. Hispano folklife of New Mexico: the Lorin W. Brown Federal Writers' Project manuscripts. Albuquerque, University of New Mexico Press, c1978. xiii, 279 p. illus.   GR104.B76
    Bibliographic references included in "Notes" (p. 253-258).
    Appendix: "Notes on Federal Project Number One and the Federal Writers' Project in New Mexico": p. 239-252.
    Manuscripts have undergone "minor editing" which is described in the preface.

357
First person America. Edited and with an introduction by Ann Banks. New York, Knopf, distributed by Random House, 1980. xxv, 287 p. illus.   E169.F56
    Bibliography: p. [273]-278.
    Eighty narratives originally recorded by members of the Federal Writers' Project.

358
Such as us: Southern voices of the thirties. Edited by Tom E. Terrill and Jerrold Hirsch. Chapel Hill, University of North Carolina Press, c1978. xxvi, 302 p. illus.
HN79.A13S87

Selections from life histories compiled by FWP employees in the Southeast. Materials were edited and sometimes shortened as described in the introduction.

Slave Narratives
(entries are arranged
in chronological order)

359
Federal Writers' Project. Slave narratives: a folk history of slavery in the United States from interviews with former slaves. Washington, D.C., 1941. 17 v. in 33. mounted photos.   E444.F27 Rare Bk Coll
    Contents: v. 1. Alabama narratives.—v. 2. Arkansas narratives.—v. 3. Florida narratives.—v. 4. Georgia narratives.—v. 5. Indiana narratives.—v. 6. Kansas narratives.—v. 7. Kentucky narratives.—v. 8. Maryland narratives.— v. 9. Mississippi narratives.—v. 10. Missouri narratives.—v. 11. North Carolina narratives.— v. 12. Ohio narratives.—v. 13. Oklahoma narratives.— v. 14. South Carolina narratives.—v. 15. Tennessee narratives.—v. 16. Texas narratives.—v. 17. Virginia narratives.
    WPA employees at the Library of Congress assembled typewritten records of interviews (made between 1936 and 1938 by FWP writers in 17 states) into bound volumes kept in the Library's Rare Book Room. The records are also available on microfilm (no. 974) in the Microform Reading Room.

360
Lay my burden down; a folk history of slavery. Edited by B. A. Botkin. Chicago, Ill., University of Chicago Press [1945] xxi, 285 p. plates.   E144.F26

An edited and topically arranged "selection of excerpts and complete narratives from the Slave Narrative Collection of the Federal Writers' Project" in the Library of Congress.

361
Yetman, Norman R., comp. Voices from slavery. [1st ed.] New York, Holt, Rinehart and Winston [c1970] 368 p. illus.
                E444.Y42
    "Selections from the Slave Narrative Collection of the Federal Writers' Project" in the Library of Congress. The material chosen received "minor editing" which is described in the introduction.
    Also issued in a paperbound edition with the title *Life Under the "Peculiar Institution"* (New York, Holt, Rinehart, and Winston [1970] E444.Y4)
    "A Photo Essay of Former Slaves" [16 leaves] is inserted between p. 338 and 339.
    "The Background of the Slave Narrative Collection" (p. 339-355) was first published in a slightly different form in the *American Quarterly,* v. 19, fall 1967, p. 534-553.

362
The American slave: a composite autobiography. Edited by George P. Rawick. Westport, Conn., Greenwood Pub. Co., 1972-73. 19 v. (Contributions in Afro-American and African studies, no. 11)
                E441.A58
    Bibliography: v. 1, p. 179-200.
    Contents: v. 1. From sundown to sunup: the making of the black community.— v. 12-3. South Carolina narratives.—v. 4-5. Texas narratives.—v. 6. Alabama and Indiana narratives.—v. 7. Oklahoma and Mississippi narratives.—v. 8-10. Arkansas

narratives.—v. 11. Arkansas narratives. Missouri narratives.—v. 12-13. Georgia narratives.—v. 14-15. North Carolina narratives.—v. 16. Kansas, Kentucky, Maryland, Ohio, Virginia, and Tennessee narratives.—v. 17. Florida narratives.—v. 18. Unwritten history of slavery (Fisk University).—v. 19. God struck me dead (Fisk University).

The first volume is an interpretive essay by George Rawick dealing with the conditions of life under slavery, into which he incorporated illustrative passages from the narratives. Appendixes to Vol. 1 include "Editor's Introduction to Volumes 2-19," front matter from the WPA's 1941 collection at the Library of Congress, and instructions to interviewers regarding interview structure and transcription in dialect. Volumes 2 through 17 are reprints of the slave narratives held in the Rare Book Collection of the Library of Congress.

- - - - - - - - - Supplement, series 1. Edited by George P. Rawick, general editor, with Jan Hillegas and Ken Lawrence, editors. Westport, Conn., Greenwood Pub. Co., 1977. 12 v. (Contributions in Afro-American and African studies, no. 35)

E444.A45 suppl. 1

Contents: v. 1. Alabama narratives.—v. 2. Arkansas, Colorado, Minnesota, Missouri, and Oregon and Washington narratives.—v. 3-4. Georgia narratives.— v. 5. Indiana and Ohio narratives.—v. 6-10. Mississippi narratives.—v. 11. North Carolina and South Carolina narratives.—v. 12. Oklahoma narratives.

Rawick and his associates became involved in the search for additional narratives not included in the LC's Rare Book Collection and enlisted the cooperation of archives, historical societies and other de-positories around the country. The material was transcribed by typists before it was reproduced here. In his "General Intro-dution" (p. [ix]-xlviii) Rawick discusses the problems associated with using the narratives for historical scholarship.

- - - - - - - - - - Supplement, series 2. George P. Rawick, general editor. Westport, Conn., Greenwood Press, 1979. 10 v. (Contributions in Afro-American and African studies, no. 49)   E444.A45 suppl. 2

Contents: v. 1. Alabama, Arizona, Arkansas, District of Columbia, Florida, Georgia, Indiana, Kansas, Maryland, Nebraska, New York, North Carolina, Oklahoma, Rhode Island, South Carolina, Washington narratives.—v. 2-10. Texas narratives.

Rawick concludes that all known narratives collected by WPA interviewers have now been published in his volumes and those compiled by other editors, with the exception of some remaining Florida and Louisiana papers that are currently being prepared for publication.

363
Woodward, Comer Vann. History from slave sources; a review article. American historical review, v. 79, Apr. 1974: 470-481.   E171.A57, v. 79

While reviewing *The American Slave: A Composite Autobiography,* edited by George P. Rawick, Woodward describes the interviews with former slaves collected by the FWP and discusses their reliability as source material for histories of slavery in America.

364
Weevils in the wheat: interviews with Virginia ex-slaves. Edited by Charles L.

Perdue, Jr., Thomas E. Barden and Robert K. Phillips. Charlottesville, University Press of Virginia, 1976. xiv, 405 p. illus.

E444.V57

"A collection of interviews of former slaves, conducted by the Virginia Federal Writers' Project in 1936 and 1937." George P. Rawick designates this publication a "definitive collection" that supplements his own volumes.

365

Federal Writers' Project. Slave narratives: a folk history of slavery in the United States from interviews with former slaves. St. Clair Shores, Mich., Scholarly Press, 1976. 17 v.   E444.F27 1976 Folk

Reprint of the typewritten records prepared by the Federal Writers' Project, 1936-1938, assembled by the Library of Congress project, Work Projects Administration for the District of Columbia. In some cases material from two or more states was combined into a single volume.

Contents: v. 1-2. South Carolina narratives.—v. 3-4. Texas narratives.—v. 5. Alabama and Indiana narratives.—v. 6. Oklahoma and Mississippi narratives.— v. 7-9. Arkansas narratives.—v. 10. Arkansas narratives. Missouri narratives.— v. 11-12. Georgia narratives.—v. 13-14. North Carolina narratives.—v. 15. Kansas, Kentucky, and Maryland narratives.—v. 16. Ohio, Virginia, and Tennessee narratives.—v. 17. Florida narratives.

HISTORICAL RECORDS SURVEY

In 1942 Sargent Child, in his article "What Is Past Is Prologue," reported that 1,940 publications of the HRS had been published and the number was expected to reach 2,000. At the Library of Congress the published reports of the HRS are filed under "Historical Records Survey" followed by the individual state name.

Child also noted that "It is quite apparent to those who have examined the final inventories of the files . . . that ten times as much inventory and research material has been collected and placed in orderly arrangement as has been published." Much of this unpublished material was left in state depositories. Since one mission of the HRS was to bring order to the chaos of local record control, it is ironic that its own records of the records were to suffer a similar fate. Many of the unpublished records of the HRS have been shuffled, lost, rearranged, or destroyed, despite the efforts of scholars to reclaim them.

Guides and Comments

366

Child, Sargent B., and Dorothy P. Holmes. Check list of Historical Records Survey publications. Baltimore, Genealogical Pub. Co., 1969. 110 p. (W.P.A. Technical series. Research and records bibliography no. 7)   Z1223.Z7C52 MRR Alc

Reprint of the 1943 edition.

367

Child, Sargent B. What is past is prologue. American archivist, v. 5, Oct. 1942: 217-227.   CD3020.A45, v. 5

A similar report by the same author with the same title was issued in Newark, by the Historical Records Survey in 1942 (24 p. CD3020.H6C47) with two appendixes. Appendix II (p. 24), "Inventories Published by the Historical Records Survey," presents tabular data chronologically arranged by type of inventory.

Evaluates the scope of the achievement of the HRS, and argues that the project must be revived after the war, finding it "inconceivable that there will be permanently discontinued an undertaking which, beyond question, has been the largest scale project of its nature ever undertaken by any nation at any time and which has produced in spite of obvious shortcomings, a remarkably valuable result."

368
Harrell, Mary E. comp. W.P.A. church survey. In Cincinnati Historical Society. Bulletin, v. 24, July 1966: 236-248. illus.
　　　　　　　　F486.H653, v. 24
Excerpts from the Society's WPA files describing churches in Cincinnati.

369
Hoyt, Max E. Unpublished Historical Records Survey inventories. In National Genealogical Society. Quarterly, v. 33, June 1945: 33-35.　　　CS42.N4, v. 33
Describes the inventories of unpublished survey material compiled in about two-thirds of the states and adds some omitted titles for Maine to the Child and Holmes list (no. 364).

370
Portner, Stuart. Report on the status of the files of the Michigan Historical Records Survey, 1936-42. Michigan history magazine, v. 27, Oct./Dec. 1943: 707-726.
　　　　　　　　F561.M57, v. 27

371
Rapport, Leonard. Dumped from a wharf into Casco Bay: the Historical Records Survey revisited. American archivist, v. 37, Apr. 1974: 201-210.　CD3020.A45, v. 37

An account of some of the adventures and frustrations he met while trying to locate unpublished HRS materials.

372
The W.P.A. Historical Records Survey: a guide to the unpublished inventories, indexes, and transcripts. Compiled by Loretta L. Hefner. Chicago, Society of American Archivists, 1980, 42 p.
Not yet available at LC.
"Suggested Reading List": p. 8; "A Guide to the Unpublished Historical Records Survey Materials in Each State": p. 9-37; "Detailed Lists of Counties, Municipalities, and Denominations" on microfiche card inserted in the inside back cover.

Bibliography of American Literature

373
Literary writings in America: a bibliography. Millwood, N.Y., KTO Press, 1977. 8 v.
　　　　　　　　Z1225.L58 MRR Alc
Work on a bibliography of American literature was carried on at the University of Pennsylvania where WPA/HRS workers reviewed "over 2,000 volumes of periodicals, more than 500 volumes of literary history and criticism, and more than 100 bibliographies" to find material by and about a wide range of American authors. In 1976 KTO Press began publication of the card file which had been preserved at the University of Pennsylvania's Charles Patterson Van Pelt Library. "The present volumes, which are the result of photo-offsetting the entire card catalog, represent the file as it existed when the project was terminated in 1942."

American Imprints Inventory

More than forty volumes of the American Imprints Inventory were published before the termination of the project. Another 15 or so were nearing completion. In the Library of Congress references to the published works are filed under "Historical Records Survey. American Imprints Inventory."

The nearly 15 million book slips collected by project workers were given to the custody of the Library of Congress. Through the years researchers have worked in the files compiling regional and chronological checklists as books and theses. No attempt has been made here to list all those works.

In 1957 the inventory slips relating to imprints before 1801 were deposited with the American Antiquarian Society in Worcester, Mass. In 1970 the remainder, in 150 or more large filing cases, was deposited at Rutgers University Library. Scarecrow Press makes extensive use of the file in compiling its Checklist of American Imprints which is described in detail below.

374

Farran, Don. American Imprints Inventory—final report, May 1, 1942. In Child, Sargent B. What is past is prologue. Newark, Historical Records Survey, 1942. Appendix I, p. 19-23.   CD3020.H6C47

375

Historical Records Survey. American imprints by date. [Catalog of entries for 1652-1905. 193-?] 5 reels.   Micro 695 Z
 Microfilm copy of catalog cards. Negative.
 Film incomplete: reel 2 for 1776-1798 wanting.

376

The Imprints Catalogue. Wisconsin magazine of history, v. 25, June 1942: 387.
                F576.W7, v. 25
 Brief note reports that the 15 million odd slips of the American Imprints Inventory (property of the Library of Congress) have been sent to the Library of the Wisconsin Historical Society for safekeeping during World War II.

377

McMurtrie, Douglas C. A list of publications issued 1937-1942 by the American Imprints Inventory of the WPA's Historical Records Survey. Evanston, Ill., 1943. 4 numbered leaves.   Z1215.M2

Checklist of American Imprints
(entries in chronological order)

378

Shaw, Ralph R., and Richard H. Shoemaker. American bibliography, a preliminary checklist for 1801-1819. New York, Scarecrow Press, 1958-66. 22 v.   Z1215.S48
 Contents: v. 1-19. Items 1-50192.—v. 20. Addenda, list of sources, library symbols.—[v. 21] Title index.—v. 22. Corrections; author index.

379

Shoemaker, Richard H. A checklist of American imprints for 1820-1829. New York, Scarecrow Press, 1964-71. 10 v.
                Z1215.S5
 Vols. for 1826-1829 compiled by Richard H. Shoemaker assisted by Gayle Cooper.
 Vols. for 1821-1829 published in Metuchen, N.J.

- - - - - - - - - - Title index, compiled by M. Frances Cooper. Metuchen, N.J., Scarecrow Press, 1972. 556 p.

Z1215.S5 Suppl.

- - - - - - - - - - Author index; corrections & sources, compiled by M. Frances Cooper. Metuchen, N.J., Scarecrow Press, 1973. 172 p. Z1215.S5 Suppl. 2

380

A Checklist of American imprints. 1830+ Metuchen, N.J., Scarecrow Press, 1972+

Z1215.C44

Compilers: 1830, Gayle Cooper.— 1831+, Scott Bruntjen and Carol Bruntjen.

While it was the intent of the compilers to produce as full a list as possible of American books published in the early 19th century, and not simply to reproduce the voluminous files of the American Imprints Inventory, they acknowledge their dependence on the original work of the WPA and in many instances include its citations without verification. Thus, much of the unpublished work of the imprints inventory is gradually being made available.

FEDERAL THEATRE PROJECT

A large body of uncataloged material associated with the FTP was accumulated at the Library of Congress following the death of the project. Space limitations forced the transfer of the material to warehouse storage where it remained until 1975 when the Library and George Mason University worked out an arrangement so that the collection would be sent on permanent loan to the university for research purposes.

Lorraine Brown described her first impression of the material. "We found six thousand play and radio scripts, dozens of cabinets of photographs, production notebooks, and play reader reports, crates of posters and set and costume designs, and even seven file cabinets full of newspaper clippings that were the base of the living newspaper morgue."

This collection formed the nucleus of the university's Research Center for the Federal Theatre. Aided by a grant from the National Endowment for the Humanities, center personnel have sorted and classified the material and supplemented it with additional collections and oral history interviews with former project participants.

381

Brown, Lorraine. A story yet to be told: the Federal Theatre research project. Black scholar, v. 11, July/Aug. 1979: 70-78.

E185.5.B575, v. 11

382

Federal One. v. 1+, 1976+ Fairfax, Va., Research Center for the Federal Theatre Project, George Mason University.

Frequency varies. N&CPR

GRR Bibl

A mimeographed newsletter describing activity and new developments at the Research Center. Included are accounts of visitors and their research projects, descriptions of acquisitions, and articles based on research in the collections.

383

Free, adult, uncensored: the living history of the Federal Theatre Project. Edited by John O'Connor and Lorraine Brown.

Foreword by John Houseman. Washington, New Republic Books; New York, trade distributions by Simon and Schuster, 1978. [228] p. illus.   PN2266.F66

Illustrations include reproductions of photographs, handbills, costume sketches, and set designs found in the collection of FWP material now housed at George Mason University.

384

WPA collection available [at George Mason University Library] American libraries, v. 6, Mar. 1975: 142.   Z673.A5B82, v. 6

Appendix I

Doctoral Dissertations

Adubato, Robert A. A history of the WPA's Negro Theatre Project in New York City, 1935-1939. (Ph.D., New York University, 1978. 369 p.)

Abstracted in *Dissertation Abstracts International*, v. 39A, Oct. 1978, p. 1930 (DDK 78-20481).

Argersinger, Jo Ann Eady. Baltimore: the Depression years. (Ph.D., The George Washington University, 1980. 362 p.)

Abstracted in *Dissertation Abstracts International*, v. 41A, July 1980, p. 349 (8014054).

Arthur, Thomas Hahn. The political career of an actor: Melvyn Douglas and the New Deal. (Ph.D., Indiana University, 1973. 216 p.)

Abstracted in *Dissertation Abstracts International*, v. 34A, Mar. 1974, p. 5850 (DCJ 74-07000).

Barrese, Edward Francis. The Historical Records Survey: a nation acts to save its memory. (Ph.D., The George Washington University, 1980. 180 p.)

Abstracted in *Dissertation Abstracts International*, v. 41A, Nov. 1980, p. 2180 (8023846).

Berman, Greta. The lost years: mural painting in New York City under the Works Progress Administration's Federal Art Project, 1935-1943. (Ph.D., Columbia University, 1975. 437 p.)

Abstracted in *Dissertation Abstracts International*, v. 36A, Dec. 1975, p. 3174 (DCJ 75-27379).

Billings, Alan Gailey. Design in the Works Progress Administration's Federal Theatre Project (1935 to 1939). (Ph.D., University of Illinois, 1967. 184 p.)

Abstracted in *Dissertation Abstracts*, v. 28A, Oct. 1967, p. 1550 (67-11823).

Blumberg, Barbara Marilyn. The Works Progress Administration in New York City: a case study of the New Deal in action. (Ph.D., Columbia University, 1974. 623 p.)

Abstracted in *Dissertation Abstracts International*, v. 35A, Apr. 1974, p. 6624 (DCJ 75-07476).

Blumell, Bruce Dudley. The development of public assistance in the State of Washington during the Great Depression. (Ph.D., University of Washington, 1973. 497 p.)

Abstracted in *Dissertation Abstracts International*, v. 34A, Jan. 1974, p. 4138 (DCJ 74-00786).

Cannon, Cornelius B. The Federal Music Project of the Works Progress Administration: music in a democracy. (Ph. D., University of Minnesota, 1963. 320 p.)

Abstracted in *Dissertation Abstracts*, v. 24, Nov. 1963, p. 2068 (63-7915).

Carr, Eleanor M. The New Deal and the sculptor: a study of federal relief to the sculptor on the New York City Federal Art Project of the Works Progress Administration, 1935-1943. (Ph.D., New York University, 1969. 246 p.)

Abstracted in *Dissertation Abstracts International*, v. 30A, Feb. 1970, p. 3389 (70-03048).

Clayton, Ronnie Wayne. A history of the Federal Writers' Project in Louisiana.

(Ph.D., Louisiana State University, 1974. 364 p.)

Abstracted in *Dissertation Abstracts International,* v. 35A, Nov. 1974, p. 2891 (DCJ 74-24765).

Contreras, Belisario Ramon. The New Deal Treasury Department art programs and the American artist, 1933 to 1943. (Ph.D., The American University, 1967. 394 p.)

Abstracted in *Dissertation Abstracts,* v. 28A, Oct. 1967, p. 1356 (67-12035).

Dunfee, Charles Dennis. Harold H. Burton, Mayor of Cleveland: the WPA program, 1935-1937. (Ph.D., Case Western Reserve University, 1975. 387 p.)

Abstracted in *Dissertation Abstracts International,* v. 37A, July 1976, p. 543 (DCJ 76-16039).

Dycke, Marjorie L. The Living Newspaper: a study of the nature of the form and its place in modern social drama. (Ph.D., New York University, 1948. 183 p.)

Abstracted in *Microfilm Abstracts,* v. 9, no. 1, 1949, p. 30-32 (00-01127).

Frank, Felicia Nina Liss. The magazines "Workers Theatre," "New Theatre" and "New Theatre and Film" as documents of the American left-wing theatre movement of the nineteen-thirties. (Ph.D., City University of New York, 1976. 515 p.)

Abstracted in *Dissertation Abstracts International,* v. 37A, Dec. 1976, p. 3273 (DCJ 76-28271).

Goodson, Martia Graham. An introductory essay and subject index to selected interviews from the slave narrative collection. (Ph.D., Union Graduate School [Ohio], 1977. 132 p.)

Abstracted in *Dissertation Abstracts International,* v. 38A, Mar. 1978, p. 5647 (DDK 78-00120).

Hammouda, Abdul-Aziz Abdul-Salam Soliman. The Living Newspaper: a study in source and form. (Ph.D., Cornell University, 1968. 157 p.)

Abstracted in *Dissertation Abstracts,* v. 29A, Dec. 1968, p. 1978 (68-16178).

Hanson, James Austin. The Civilian Conservation Corps in the northern Rocky Mountains. (Ph.D., University of Wyoming, 1973. 404 p.)

Abstracted in *Dissertation Abstracts International,* v. 34A, June 1974, p. 7677 (74-13289).

Kifer, Allen Francis. The Negro under the New Deal, 1933-1941. (Ph.D., The University of Wisconsin, 1961. 303 p.)

Abstracted in *Dissertation Abstracts,* v. 22, Sept. 1961, p. 852 (61-03124).

Kramp, Robert Scott. The Great Depression: its impact on forty-six large American public libraries, an inquiry based on a content analysis of published writings of their directors. (Ph.D., The University of Michigan, 1975. 227 p.)

Abstracted in *Dissertation Abstracts International,* v. 36A, Dec. 1975, p. 3188 (DCJ 75-29266).

Lally, Kathleen Ann. A history of the Federal Dance Theatre of the Works Progress Administration, 1935-1939. (Ph.D., Texas Woman's University, 1978. 110 p.)

Abstracted in *Dissertation Abstracts International,* v. 40A, July 1979, p. 6 (DEL 79-15877).

Lashbrook, Lawrence Gene. Work relief in Maine: the administration and programs of the WPA. (Ph.D., University of Maine, 1977. 263 p.)

Abstracted in *Dissertation Abstracts International*, v. 38A, Mar. 1978, p. 5660 (DDK 78-01696).

Leff, Mark Hugh. The New Deal and taxation, 1933-1939: the limits of symbolic reform. (Ph.D., University of Chicago, 1978)

Abstracted in *Dissertation Abstracts International*, v. 39A, Apr. 1979, p. 6298.

Lofton, Paul S. A social and economic history of Columbia, South Carolina, during the Great Depression, 1929-1940. (Ph.D., University of Texas at Austin, 1977. 346 p.)

Abstracted in *Dissertation Abstracts International*, v. 38A, Jan. 1978, p. 4330 (DDK 77-29061).

McElvaine, Robert Stuart. Thunder without lightning: working class discontent in the United States, 1929-1937. (Ph.D., State University of New York at Binghampton, 1974. 338 p.)

Abstracted in *Dissertation Abstracts International*, v. 35A, Oct. 1974, p. 2182 (DCJ 74-20701).

McKinzie, Kathleen O'Connor. Writers on relief: 1935-1942. (Ph.D., Indiana University, 1970. 290 p.)

Abstracted in *Dissertation Abstracts International*, v. 31A, Nov. 1970, p. 2316 (70-22834).

McKinzie, Richard D. The New Deal for artists: federal subsidies, 1933 to 1943. (Ph.D., Indiana University, 1969. 331 p.)

Abstracted in *Dissertation Abstracts International*, v. 30A, Sept. 1969, p. 1113 (69-14712).

Marcello, Ronald Ely. The North Carolina Works Progress Administration and the politics of relief. (Ph.D., Duke University, 1969. 280 p.)

Abstracted in *Dissertation Abstracts International*, v. 30A, Oct. 1969, p. 1505 (69-16760).

Marling, Karal Ann Rose. Federal patronage and the Woodstock [Art] Colony. (Ph.D., Bryn Mawr College, 1971. 594 p.)

Abstracted in *Dissertation Abstracts International*, v. 32A, Apr. 1972, p. 5687 (72-11201).

Mathews, Jane DeHart. Art, relief, and politics: the federal theatre, 1935-1939. (Ph.D., Duke University, 1966. 403 p.)

Abstracted in *Dissertation Abstracts*, v. 28A, Aug. 1967, p. 600 (67-09753).

Mendoza, Barbara Murphy. Hallie Flanagan: her role in American theatre, 1924-1935. (Ph.D., New York University, 1976. 500 p.)

Abstracted in *Dissertation Abstracts International*, v. 37A, Mar. 1977, p. 5444 (DCJ 77-05322).

Miller, M. Lawrence. Original federal theatre protest plays—1936-1939: New Deal contributions to the American drama of social concern. (Ph.D., University of California, Los Angeles, 1968. 237 p.)

Abstracted in *Dissertation Abstracts*, v. 29A, Apr. 1969, p. 3616 (69-05336).

Monroe, Gerald M. The artists union of New York. (Ed.D., New York University, 1971. 287 p.)

Abstracted in *Dissertations Abstracts International*, v. 32A, Nov. 1971, p. 2576 (71-28586).

Penkower, Monty Noam. The Federal Writers' Project: a study in government patronage of the arts. (Ph.D., Columbia University, 1970).

Penrod, John A. American literature and the Great Depression. (Ph.D., University of Pennsylvania, 1954. 290 p.)
    Abstracted in *Dissertation Abstracts*, v. 14, [Sept.] 1954, p. 1419 (00-08572).

Pietan, Norman. Federal government and the arts. (Ph.D., Columbia University, 1950. 334 p.)
    Abstracted in *Microfilm Abstracts*, v. 11, no. 2, 1951, p. 217 (00-02351).

Rabkin, Gerald Edward. Drama and political commitment: the impact of politics on American drama of the 1930's. (Ph.D., The Ohio State University, 1961. 460 p.)
    Abstracted in *Dissertation Abstracts*, v. 22, Aug. 1961, p. 575 (61-02842).

Rader, Frank John. Harry L. Hopkins: the Works Progress Administration and national defense, 1935-1940. (Ph.D., University of Delaware, 1973. 256 p.)
    Abstracted in *Dissertation Abstracts International*, v. 34A, Apr. 1974, p. 6573 (DCJ 74-08742).

Ridge, Patricia Lin. The contributions of Hallie Flanagan to the American theatre. (Ph.D., University of Colorado, 1971. 167 p.)
    Abstracted in *Dissertation Abstracts International*, v. 32A, Jan. 1972, p. 4161 (72-03695).

Rubenstein, Erica Beckh. Tax payers murals. (Ph.D., Radcliffe College, 1944. 742 p.)

Sherwood, Leland Harley. The federal sponsored community art centers of Iowa as a part of the New Deal. (Ed.D., Indiana University, 1973. 212 p.)
    Abstracted in *Dissertation Abstracts International*, v. 34A, Feb. 1974, p. 4581 (DCJ 74-02704).

Smith, Douglas Lloyd. The New Deal and the urban South: the advancement of a Southern urban consciousness during the Depression decade. (Ph.D., University of Southern Mississippi, 1978. 590 p.)
    Abstracted in *Dissertation Abstracts International*, v. 39A, Apr. 1979, p. 6300 (DEL 79-05148).

Starling, Marion Wilson. The slave narrative: its place in American literary history. (Ph.D., New York University, 1946. 292 p.)

Taber, Ronald Warren. The Federal Writers' Project in the Pacific Northwest: a case study (Ph.D., Washington State University, 1969. 196 p.)
    Abstracted in *Dissertation Abstracts International*, v. 30A, Apr. 1970, p. 4389 (70-05681).

Warren-Findley, Jannelle Jedd. Of tears and need: the Federal Music Project, 1935-1943. (Ph.D., The George Washington University, 1973.)

Weir, Jean Burwell. Timberline Lodge; a WPA experiment in architecture and crafts. (Ph.D., The University of Michigan, 1977. 2 v. 513 p.)

Abstracted in *Dissertation Abstracts International,* v. 38A, May 1978, p. 6363 (DDK 78-04838).

Werthman, Joan B. The New Deal federal art programs, 1935-1939. (Ph.D., St. John's University, 1971. 265 p.)
Abstracted in *Dissertation Abstracts International,* v. 33A, Aug. 1972, p. 7130 (72-21739).

Williams, Colleen Ingram. Work relief as a social service delivery system: the experience of the WPA, 1935-1942. (D.S.W., Tulane University School of Social Work, 1976. 328 p.)
Abstracted in *Dissertation Abstracts International,* v. 37A, Nov. 1976, p. 3191 (DCJ 76-25353).

Woodworth, William H. The Federal Music Project of the Works Progress Administration in New Jersey. (Ed.D., The University of Michigan, 1970. 215 p.)
Abstracted in *Dissertation Abstracts International,* v. 31A, Feb. 1971, p. 4211 (71-4550).

Appendix II

Some WPA Administrators

This list is provided as an aid for users of the bibliography. No pretense is made to completeness, nor was any attempt made to indicate the many different positions one person may have held in the WPA management hierarchy.

ABBOTT, Bernice	1938?	FAP	Director, New York photographic project
ABBOTT, Leonard	1935	FWP	National office, Research Editor
ABT, John J.	1935	WPA	Assistant General Counsel
ALGREN, Nelson	1938	FWP	Supervisor, Chicago folklore unit
ALSBERG, Henry	1935	FWP	National Director
ANDERSON, Nels	1938	WPA	Director, Labor Relations Section
ANDREASSEN, John C. L.	1937?	HRS	Regional Supervisor
ASHER, Robert	1935	WPA	Assistant, Federal One Finance Office
ASKLING, John	1935	FTP	Executive Director, New York City region
BAKER, Jacob	1935	WPA	Assistant Administrator
BARBER, Philip	1935	FTP	Regional Director
BARKER, Burt Brown	1935	FAP	Field Supervisor
BEAR, Donald	1935	FAP	Field Supervisor
BELL, Ulric R.	1938	FWP	Director, Kentucky project
BILLINGTON, Ray A.	1936	FWP	Director, Massachusetts project
BJORKMAN, Edwin	1938	FWP	Director, North Carolina project
BOSWORTH, Francis	1936	FTP	Director, National Play Bureau
BOTKIN, Benjamin A.	1935	FWP	National office, Folklore Editor
BRODIE, Mabel S.	1938	HRS	National office, Editor, public records unit
BROWN, Gilmore	1935	FTP	Regional Director
BROWN, Sterling A.	1937	FWP	National office, Editor of Negro Affairs
BROWNE, Waldo R.	1935	FWP	National office, Literary Editor
BUFANO, Remo	1936	FTP	Director, New York City marionette unit
CAHILL, Holger	1935	FAP	National Director
CARMODY, John M.	1939	FWA	Administrator
CARNES, Eva M.	1935	HRS	State Director, West Virginia
CHADBOURNE, Horace	1935	FWP	Assistant Director, South Dakota project
CHILD, Sargent P.	1939	HRS	National Director
CHOATES, Grace Stone	1935	FWP	Assistant Director, Montana project
CHRISTGAU, Victor	1939	WPA	State Administrator, New Jersey
CLIFTON, Chalmers	1935	FMP	Director, New York City unit
CLINE, Dorothy I.	1937	WPA	Training Consultant to Recreation Section
COLBY, Merle	1937	FWP	National office, Territorial Editor
COLGAN, Howard E.	1935	HRS	Assistant to the Director
CONNOLLY, Donald	1938	WPA	State Administrator, California
COOPER, Charlotte G.	1935	FAP	State Director, Ohio
CORNELIUS, Charles O.	1936	FAP	Supervisor, New York City Index of American Design
CORNELL, Louis	1936	FMP	Assistant to the National Director

COUCH, William Terry	1935	FWP	Regional Director
COY, Harold	1935?	FWP	National office, Executive Editor
CRONIN, Agnes N.	1936	WPA	Administrative Assistant, Women's and Professional Division
CRONYN, George	1935	FWP	Associate National Director
CUNNINGHAM, William	1935	FWP	Director, Oklahoma project
CURRAN, Mary	1935	FAP	Field Supervisor
DANYSH, Joseph	1935	FAP	Field Supervisor
DAVIDSON, Julius	1937	WPA	Finance Officer, Federal One
DAVIS, E. Kendall	1936	FTP	Field advisor to national office
DAVIS, J. Frank	1935?	FWP	Director, Texas project
DEETER, Jasper	1935	FTP	Regional Director
DEFENBACHER, Daniel S.	1935	FAP	State Director, North Carolina
DILLARD, Henry B.	1941	HRS	Supervisor, District of Columbia
DORNBUSH, Adrian	1939?	Art	National office, Director of arts and crafts
DORT, Dallas W.	1936?	WPA	Director, Division of Investigation
DOTEN, Dana	1935?	FWP	State Director, Vermont project
DOWLING, Eddie	1935?	FTP	Director of vaudeville
DREYER, Edward P.	1938	FWP	Assistant Director, Louisiana project
DU BOSE, Louise Jones	1935?	FWP	Assistant Director, South Carolina project
DUNN, J. W.	1935	WPA	State Administrator, Oklahoma
EDWARDS, Elizabeth	1936	HRS	National office, Editor, federal archives inventory unit
EDWARDS, Paul	1937	WPA	Administrative Officer for Federal One in New York City
EGAN, James W.	1935	FWP	Director, Washington state project
ELIOT, Margaret S.	1937	HRS	National office staff
EVANS, Luther H.	1935	HRS	National Director
FARNSWORTH, William P.	1936	FTP	Assistant National Director
FISHER, Vardis	1935?	FWP	Director, Idaho project
FLANAGAN, Hallie	1935	FTP	National Director
FOSTER, George	1940	FMP	Deputy Director
FRANK, Yasha	1938	FTP	National Consultant for the children's theater
FREDENHAGEN, Dorothy	1935	FMP	National office staff
FREDERICK, John T.	1935	FWP	Director, Illinois project
FRENCH, Paul Comly	1936	FWP	Director, Pennsylvania project
FUHLBRUEGGE, Irene	1936	FWP	Director, New Jersey project
GABLE, J. Harris	1938	FWP	Director, Nebraska project
GAER, Joseph	1935	FWP	Field Supervisor
GATTS, George	1935	FTP	Assistant Regional Director
GERWING, George	1937	FTP	State Director, California

GIBBS, Dwight, W.	1938	FTP	Architectural Consultant
GILDER, Rosamund	1935	FTP	Director, Bureau of Research and Publications
GILL, Corrington.	1938	WPA	Assistant Administrator
GLASSGOLD, C. Adolph	1936	FAP	National Coordinator, Index of American Design
GOLDSCHMIDT, Arthur	1935	WPA	Federal One planning committee
GRAHAM, Shirley	1936?	FTP	Director, Negro unit in Chicago
GRAY, Roland P.	1935?	FWP	Research editor in New York state
GREGORIE, Anne K.	1935	HRS	State Director, South Carolina
GRIFFITH, E. J.	1935	WPA	State Administrator, Oregon
GROCE, George G.	1940	HRS	National consultant for the portrait survey
HAHN, Theodore	1938	FMP	State Director, Ohio
HALPERT, Edith G.	1936	FAP	Assistant to Director, exhibitions section
HALPERT, Herbert	1937?	FTP	Director, National Service Bureau.
HARLAN, Hugh	1935	FWP	Director, Los Angeles unit
HARRINGTON, Francis C.	1938	WPA	Administrator
HARRIS, Reed	1935	FWP	Assistant Director
HARTOG, Alfred	1938	FWP	Supervisor, living-lore unit of New York City
HATCHER, Harlan	1938	FWP	Director, Ohio project
HAWK, Muriel	1937	FWP	Director, Massachusetts project
HETTWER, Dora Thea	1935	FWP	Executive secretary to national director
HEWES, Harry L.	1937?	FMP	National office, Index of American Composers
HOKE, Travis	1937	FWP	Director, New York City project
HOLT, Thad	1936	WPA	Assistant Administrator in charge of Division of Employment
HOLZHAUER, Mildred	1935	FAP	Exhibition management
HOPKINS, Harry	1935	WPA	Administrator
HOPPER, James	1935	FWP	Director, California project
HOUSEMAN, John	1936	FTP	Co-Director, Negro unit, New York City
HUGHES, Gareth	1937	FTP	Director, Los Angeles unit
HUGHES, Glenn	1935	FTP	Regional Director
HUNTER, Howard	1940	WPA	Commissioner
JOHNS, Orrick	1935	FWP	Director, New York City unit
JOHNSON, Hugh C.	1935	WPA	State Administrator, New York
JONES, Edward N.	1935	WPA	State Administrator, Pennsylvania
KELLOCK, Katharine	1936?	FWP	National office, Editor, tours section
KERR, Florence	1938	WPA	Director, Women's and Professional Division
KERR, Margaret	1937	FMP	National office staff
KLEM, Margaret	1935	WPA	Field representative, Professional and Service Division
KNOTTS, Benjamin	1940	FAP	Assistant to Director, Index of American Design.
KOCH, Frederick, H.	1935	FTP	Regional Director
KONDOLF, George	1935	FTP	State Director, Illinois

LACY, Dan	1937?	HRS	Regional Supervisor
LANG, Lester	1935	FTP	National office
LANING, Claire	1938	FWP	Assistant Director, national office
LAVERY, Emmet	1937	FTP	Director, National Service Bureau
LINDSAY, Arnett G.	1939	HRS	Supervisor, Inventory of Negro manuscripts
LOWE, K. Elmo	1935	FTP	Assistant Regional Director
MABIE, E. C.	1935	FTP	Assistant to the Director
McCLENDON, Rose	1935	FTP	Co-Director, Negro Theatre Project, New York
McCLURE, Bruce	1935	WPA	Director of Professional and Service Projects
McCONNELL, Frederick	1935	FTP	Regional Director
MacDONALD-WRIGHT, Stanton	1935	FAP	Regional Director
McFARLAND, George M.	1936	HRS	Director, Annotated Bibliography of American History
McGEE, John	1936	FTP	Field Advisor to national office
McMAHON, Audrey	1936	FAP	Director, New York City unit
McMURTRIE, Douglas C.	1936	HRS	Consultant for the imprints unit
MANGIONE, Jerre	1936?	FWP	National office, Coordinating Editor
MANUEL, Frank	1938?	FWP	Regional Director
MARCH, Frank	1936	WPA	Director, non-federal projects, Women's and Professional Division
MAYFARTH, William C.	1935	FMP	Assistant National Director
MEREDITH, Charles	1935	FTP	Regional Director
MERRIAM, Harold G.	1935	FWP	Director, Montana project
MILLER, J. Howard	1938	FTP	Deputy Director
MONSELL, Mary	1935?	FAP	National office information officer
MOODIE, Thomas H.	1937?	WPA	State Administrator, North Dakota
MOORE, Earl	1939	FMP	National Director
MORRIS, Lawrence S.	1936	WPA	Director for federal projects, Women's and Professional Division
MORRISON, Robert	1935	FAP	Assistant to national director
MOTHERWELL, Hiram	1936	FTP	Field advisor to national office
MUNSELL, Alma Sandra	1935	FMP	National office staff
MUNSON, Gorham B.	1939	FWP	Director, Library of Congress project
MYERS, Howard B.	1938	WPA	Director, Division of Social Research
NESS, Ole	1938	FTP	Regional Director
NEWSOM, John D.	1939	FWP	National Director
NILES, David K.	1936	WPA	Director of Information
NUNN, William L.	1936?	WPA	Director of Federal One in New York City
O'NEILL, Edward H.	1938	HRS	Supervisor, Bibliography of American Literature
OTTAWAY, Ruth Haller	1935	FMP	National office staff
OZER, Solomon D.	1935	WPA	Finance officer, Federal One

PARKER, Geraldine	1935	FWP	Director, Missouri project
PARKER, Thomas C.	1935	FAP	Assistant Director
PATTISON, Edward	1936	FMP	New York City Director
PERRY, Mary B.	1936	FWP	Director, New Mexico project
PRICE, Herbert S.	1936	FTP	National consultant on community drama
RADIN, Paul	1935	FWP	Regional editor
RAUCH, Frederick R.	1939	WPA	Assistant Administrator, employment
REESE, Lisle	1935	FWP	Director, South Dakota project
REEVES, Ruth	1935	FAP	National Coordinator, Index of American Design
RICE, Elmer	1935	FTP	Regional Director
RICH, Thaddeus	1936	FMP	Assistant to the national director
RIDDER, Victor	1936	WPA	Administrator, New York City
ROBERTS, Evan	1936	FTP	Director of radio division
ROBINSON, Mrs. Increase	1935	FAP	Assistant to the national director
ROHAN, Pierre de	1935?	FTP	Editor
ROSENBERG, Harold	1936?	FWP	National office, Art Editor
ROSS, Emerson	1940	WPA	Director, Division of Statistics
ROURKE, Constance	1936	FAP	Research Editor, Index of American Design
SANTEE, Ross	1938	FWP	Director, Arizona project
SAXON, Lyle	1935?	FWP	Director, Louisiana project
SCAMMELL, J. Marius	1936	HRS	Field Supervisor
SCHLAFER, Sylvia	1937?	HRS	Massachusetts portrait survey
SCHLASINGER, Ethel	1935	FWP	Director, North Dakota project
SCHOENI, Helen	1935	FTP	Assistant Regional Director
SEEGER, Charles	1938	FTP	Assistant to the director
SEIDENBERG, Roderick	1936	FWP	National office editor and field representative
SHEEHAN, Elizabeth	1935	FWP	Director, Nebraska project
SHIPTON, Clifford K.	1935	FWP	Director, Massachusetts project
SINGEWALD, Karl	1935	FWP	Director, Maryland project
SISSON, Logan B.	1935	FWP	Director, Pennsylvania project
SLOVER, Robert H.	1937	HRS	Regional Supervisor
SNOW, Taylor H.	1936	FTP	Administrative Assistant
SOKOLOFF, Nikolai	1935	FMP	National Director
SOMERVELL, Brehon	1938	WPA	Administrator, New York City
SPRING, Agnes Wright	1938?	FWP	Director, Wyoming project
STEIN, Harold	1937	WPA	Administrative officer, Federal One
STEPHENSON, Margaret	1939	WPA	Special assistant, Division of Professional and Service Projects
STEVENS, Thomas Wood	1936	FTP	Field advisor to national office
STONE, Donald C.	1935	WPA	Special assistant
TALBOT, Clarence	1936	FTP	State Director, Iowa project
THOMPSON, Donald A.	1936	HRS	National office, Editor, church records unit
THORP, George	1936	FAP	State Director, Illinois

ULRICH, Mabel S.	1935?	FWP	Director, Minnesota project
UMLAND, Rudolph	1938	FWP	Assistant State Director, Nebraska project
USSHER, Bruno David	1936	FMP	Assistant to the national director
WATKINS, C. Law	1935	FAP	Field Supervisor
WATSON, Morris	1936	FTP	Producer of the Living Newspaper
WEINER, Edythe	1936	HRS	National office, Editor, county archives unit
WESTALL, Dorris May	1936?	FWP	Director, Maine project
WESTBROOK, Lawrence	1936	WPA	Assistant Administrator
WHITE, Francis Robert	1935	FAP	State Director, Iowa
WILLIAMS, Aubrey	1938	WPA	Deputy Administrator
WOODWARD, Ellen S.	1936	WPA	Director, Women's and Professional Division

Author Index

(Numbers refer to entries, not pages.)

Colson, John Calvin, 121
Conkin, Paul K., 027
Cooper, Gayle, 379-380
Cooper, M. Frances, 379
Cordova, Gilberto Benito, 348
Cowley, Malcolm, 028, 162, 185–186
Coyle, David C., 076
Craig, Evelyn Q., 299
Cronbach, Robert, 147
Culbert, David H., 187
Current-Garcia, Eugene, 163–164

D

Davidson, Katherine H., 351
Davidson, Marshall B., 155
Davis, Edwin A., 222
Davis, Hallie Flanagan, 284–286
Denisoff, R. Serge, 277
DeVoto, Bernard, 165–166
Dieterich, Herbert R., 142
Douglass, Eri, 168
Dow, Edward F., 077
Dows, Olin, 147

E

Edel, Leon, 050
Elder, Glen H., 029
Eliot, Margaret S., 207–208
Ellis, William J., 018
Erickson, Herman, 114
Evans, Luther H., 209–217
Evans, Timothy K., 115

F

Failing, Patricia, 316
Farran, Don, 188, 243, 374
Field, Alston G., 218
Fielding, Dennis L., 319
Fiske, Harrison G., 287
Flanagan, Hallie. Search under Davis, Hallie Flanagan
Flynn, George Q., 317
Fox, Daniel M., 189
Fraenkel, Marta, 080
France, Richard, 300
Frazier, Corrine R., 081–082

G

Garoogian, Rhoda, 121
Garrett, Garet, 288
Gassner, John, 289
Gavert, Olive Lyford, 147
Gelber, Steven M., 339
Gilder, Rosamond, 290
Gill, Corrington, 007, 083
Glassgold, C. Adolph, 156
Glicksberg, Charles I., 169
Glore, Harry F., 260
Goedecke, Karl, 219
Goldstein, Harold M., 030
Goldstein, Malcolm, 302
Goldston, Robert C., 031
Gurko, Leo, 032
Gutheim, Frederick, 170

H

Hamer, Philip M., 220
Hanson, James A., 244
Harney, Andy L., 116
Harrell, Mary E., 368
Harrison, Helen A., 143
Harvey, Oswald L., 069
Hatcher, Harlan, 171
Hefner, Loretta L., 372
Hendrickson, Gordon O., 349
Hesseltine, William B., 249
Heymann, Jeanne L., 301
Hickok, Lorena A., 318
Hillegas, Jan, 362
Himelstein, Morgan Y., 303
Hirsch, Jerrold, 190, 195, 358
Hodson, William, 018
Hoffman, Paul, 339
Hogan, Willard N., 085
Hogan, William R., 225
Holcomb, Robert, 304
Hopkins, Harry L., 009–010
Hornung, Clarence P., 346
Houseman, John, 305, 383
Howard, Donald S., 086
Howard, John T., 261
Hoyt, Max E., 369

Peck, David, 320
Pells, Richard H., 042
Penkower, Monty N., 194
Perdue, Charles L., 352, 364
Perkins, John S., 097
Perry, Merrill C., 233
Peterson, Trudy H., 247
Petravage, Jacqueline, 142
Pettis, Ashley, 269
Phillips, Robert K., 352, 364
Portner, Stuart, 234, 370
Powell, Anne, 294
Purcell, Ralph, 150

R
Rabkin, Gerald, 309
Rader, Frank J., 119
Rainwater, Percy L., 235
Rapport, Leonard, 195, 371
Rauch, Basil, 043
Rawick, George P., 362
Rice, Elmer L., 310
Ring, Daniel F., 121
Roach, George W., 236–237
Robinson, Isabel J., 090
Roskolenko, Harry, 196
Ross, Ronald, 311
Rothschild, Lincoln, 147
Russell, W. Duncan, 098

S
Sawyer, Charles H., 338
Scammell, J. Marius, 238–239
Scharf, Arthur, 350
Scharf, Lois, 044
Schilling, George E., 240
Schlesinger, Arthur M., Sr., 016
Schuyler, Michael W., 045
Shaw, Ralph R., 378
Shere, Charles, 339
Shoemaker, Richard H., 378–379
Sinclair, Jo, 099
Smiley, David L., 248–249
Smiley, Sam, 312
Soapes, Thomas F., 197

Sokoloff, Nikolai, 271–273
Solman, Joseph, 147
Solomon, Izler, 279
Spaeth, Sigmund G., 280
Stanford, Edward B., 120
Stephenson, Jean, 241
Stott, William, 198
Straus, Harold, 176
Swados, Harvey, 199

T
Taber, Ronald W., 200–201
Taylor, Joshua C., 344
Terkel, Louis, 046
Terrill, Tom E., 190, 195, 358
Tonelli, Edith A., 338
Touhey, Eleanor, 177
Trout, Charles H., 047

U
Ulrich, Mabel S., 178

V
Valentine, Jerry W., 122
Van Derzee, Charlene Clay, 342
Vitz, Robert C., 152
Von Struve, A. W., 100–102

W
Walsh, Elizabeth E., 313
Warren, Frank A., 048
Warren-Findley, Jannelle J., 131, 281
Watson, Forbes, 132
Wecter, Dixon, 049
Weigle, Marta, 356
Werner, Alfred, 153
Whatley, Larry, 123
Wheeler, Burton K., 104
White, John Franklin, 121
Whitman, Willson, 295
Wilcox, Jerome K., 327–328
Wilder, Grace, 106
Williams, Edward A., 004
Williams, Jay, 314

Wilson, Edmund, 050
Wittler, Clarence J., 296
Woodward, Comer Vann, 363
Woodward, Ellen S., 107–109, 241
Woodworth, William H., 282
Worster, Donald E., 051
Wright, Roscoe, 110

Y

Yasko, Karel, 334
Yetman, Norman R., 361
Yezierska, Anzia, 202

Z

Zembala, Nancy H., 329

☆ U. S. GOVERNMENT PRINTING OFFICE: 1982 — 368-768